Cordelia C. Nevers

Wellesley Lyrics

Poems written by students and graduates of Wellesley College

Cordelia C. Nevers

Wellesley Lyrics

Poems written by students and graduates of Wellesley College

ISBN/EAN: 9783744797399

Printed in Europe, USA, Canada, Australia, Japan

Cover: Foto ©Thomas Meinert / pixelio.de

More available books at **www.hansebooks.com**

TO
THE MEMORY OF
Henry Fowle Durant
THE POET
WHOSE POEM WAS WELLESLEY COLLEGE
THIS BOOK IS LOVINGLY
Dedicated

*Ah, pause a moment! reverently listen
To one dear voice whose music lingers low
Wherever Waban's tranquil waters glisten,
   Or Waban's violets grow.*

*Where'er the cross uplifts its death-won splendor
On these fair towers, that thrilling voice is heard,
Urging, in tones unutterably tender,
   The same familiar word:*

*"Christ first, my children!"   O thou starlike spirit,
Gone with thy kindred stars to shine and burn,
May we, who now thy life and love inherit,
   Thy deepest lesson learn!*

*Christ first and last; His will our quenchless glory;
His mission ours; His service for our throne.
Why doubt we of our days' unfinished story?
   'Tis written in His own.*

—*MARION PELTON GUILD.*

Introduction.

EVERY college has its two sides. On the one hand, it is a place of lectures, libraries, laboratories, professors, studying students; a place for the acquisition of knowledge, and for increasing the extent of what is already known. Science dominates it, irrespective of temperaments, wishes, and emotions. On the other hand, it is a place where live the chosen and ardent young; where life is maturing, friendships forming, aspirations taking shape, the ideals of the home for the first time comparing themselves with those of the larger world. Here dwell hope, admiration, intimacy with noble books and persons, while gladness in these, and a daily new sense of personal power, spread everywhere an air of romance and of expanded existence. On the former of these two sides, the studious, examinations report, and the college records. Such little books as this collection of verses tell the story of the other,— the human and romantic.

For in these poems we catch sight not only of a multitude of incidents in the daily life of a company of brilliant girls, but we are permitted to know the girls themselves, to share their dreams, their friendships, their merriment, their religious aspiration, their ordered thought, natural English, and charming rhythms. He would be a hard person to please who did not enjoy society so cultured, so witty, so truly womanly, too. Let whoever fears that college life will render girls unfeminine, read and be reassured. And let him, too, read who already knows that an earnest, intellectual life furnishes the proper nutriment to vigorous health, happy dispositions, warm affections, winning graces, and devout hearts. This is the soil and these the products of the College Beautiful.

ALICE FREEMAN PALMER.

Contents.

"Agnus Dei." Josepha Virginia Sweetser	78
All Hail to the College Beautiful. Katharine Lee Bates	38
All-Hallow E'en. Agnes S. Cook	94
Alma Mater. Anne Barrett Hughes	109
Alone. Maud Thompson	71
Angelus, The. Josephine P. Simrall	40
Apart. Gertrude Spalding Henderson	114
April. Mary Russell Bartlett	74
At Sunset. Edith E. Tuxbury	129
Barriers. Helen Worthington Rogers	68
Beatrice Portinari. Mary S. Daniels	99
Birthday in Heaven, The. Mary Wright Plummer	134
Boating Song. Kent Dunlap Hägler	118
Boo! Hoo! (A Wellesley Glee)	92
By the Roadside. Louise R. Loomis	103
By Waban Banks. Lillian Corbett Barnes	124
Canterbury Tales, The. Ada May Krecker	56
Carol, A. Harriot Brewer Sterling	90
Chaucer. Mary Hollands McLean	104
Corot. Clara Brewster Potwin	139
Compensation. Alice Welch Kellogg	88
Compensation. Mabel A. Carpenter	33
Consolation. Agnes E. Wood	143
Country Children. Mary Allison Bingham	80
Crossing the Ocean. Charlotte Fitch Roberts	149
Culture. Anna Estelle Wolfson	52

Divine Right of Kings, The. Mary Wright Plummer	72
Dolores. Josepha Virginia Sweetser	54
Easter. Sara Coolidge Brooks	150
Empty Nest, The. Helen Barrett Montgomery	62
Exeunt. Lillian Corbett Barnes	97
Foiled. Sarah Chamberlin Weed	110
Four-o'clocks. Lillian B. Quinby	36
Friendship. Bertha Palmer	125
Friendship. Josephine P. Simrall	82
George Birthington's Washday. Florence E. Homer	29
Heart's Home, The. Katharine Mordantt Quint	41
Her Second Degree. Frances C. Lance	146
Hobby, A. Mabel W. White	77
H_2SO_4. Mary Eno Russell	116
Ideal, The. Katharine Lee Bates	26
Idolatry. Kent Dunlap Hägler	76
If Life were a Banquet. Josephine A. Cass	14
In Arcadie. Josephine A. Cass	57
In College Days. Florence Wilkinson	154
In Honorem: Henry F. Durant. Mary Russell Bartlett	112
In Memoriam: Helen A. Shafer. Martha Gause McCaulley	37
In the College Library. Cornelia E. Green	15
Invited by Mistake. Sarah Jane McNary	100
Irish Boat Song, An. Ambia C. Harris, Clara A. Jones	140
Isolation. Charlotte Rose Stanley	143
I Wonder if the Dying Leaf. Martha Hale Shackford	136
January in Virginia. Lillian B. Miner	93
Knighted. Mary Hollands McLean	98
Knowledge. Lillian B. Quinby	70
Lake Singer, The. Kate Watkins Tibbals	152
Lake Waban. S. Virginia Sherwood	105
Lalia. Florence Annette Wing	42
Lament of the Unathletic Maiden. Isabella Campbell	83
Lay of the Lost Hero, The. Cornelia E. Green	30

Le Pays du Tendre. Abbe Carter Goodloe	145
Life and Death. Mabel A. Carpenter	127
Love Song. Lillian Corbett Barnes	69
Love Song. Josephine P. Simrall	136
Lullaby. Emily S. Johnson	115
Mona Lisa. Abbe Carter Goodloe	17
Mr. Edward Olney, Sir. Katharine Lee Bates	120
Mutation. Mary Hefferan	19
My College Girl. Alice Welch Kellogg	64
My College Room. Mabel Wing Castle	51
My Lord the Sun. Isabella H. Fiske	102
My Own. Mary Wright Plummer	34
My Sophomore. Alice Welch Kellogg	132
Never a Day Without a Cloud. Delia Maria Taylor	151
New-Year's Wish, A. Clara Brewster Potwin	135
Night Wind in Winter, The. Martha Hale Shackford	129
October Rose, An. Clara Brewster Potwin	95
Ode. Florence Wilkinson	66
Ode on Planting the First Class Tree. Clara A. Jones	22
Ode to Ninety-Six. Mary Hefferan	87
Ode to Wellesley. Anna Robertson Brown Lindsay	25
Old Year, The. Nancy K. Foster	91
Omar Khayyam. Cornelia E. Green	73
Our College Days. Katharine Lee Bates	13
Passing Soul, The. Katharine Lee Bates	128
Picture, A. Alma E. Beale	75
Red Roses. Marion Pelton Guild	106
Rose, A. Josephine P. Simrall	108
Seaward. Ada S. Woolfolk	60
Second Thought, A. Florence Wilkinson	137
Senior's Compliment, A	144
Senior Schedule, A. Mary Hollands McLean	130
Sleeplessness. Florence Converse	50
Slender, Brown-haired Josephine	65

Shakespeare. Charlotte Rose Stanley	28
Shall I Tell You of My Lover? Theodora Kyle	148
Singer's Excuse, The. Mary Russell Bartlett	18
Song. Charlotte Rose Stanley	63
Song of Praise, A. Florence E. Homer	142
Song of Praise, A. Marion Pelton Guild	43
Song of the Lotus, The. Julia Stevens Buffington	133
Spiegel-klarheit. Anne Barrett Hughes	123
Sunset. Mary Hollands McLean	49
Tides. Josephine A. Cass	126
To ——. Mary Otis Malone	119
To an Oriole. Alma E. Beale	117
To Mt. Monadnock at Sunrise. Evangeline Kendall	96
To One I Love. Gertrude Jones	111
Touch, A. Florence Annette Wing	150
Tree-day Song, A. Annie Jerrell Tenney	138
Trust. Helen Barrett Montgomery	20
Twilight on the Hills. Anna Robertson Brown Lindsay	84
Violinist, The. Margaret Steele Anderson	16
Vivisection. Frances C. Lance	144
Waking-Time. Ada May Krecker	41
Wellesley Democracy. S.	81
When the Mist came up from the Marsh. Sarah Chamberlin Weed	89
World's Sleep, The. Sarah Chamberlin Weed	21

Wellesley Lyrics.

Our College Days.

OUR college days are over. Dost thou sigh?
    Nay, wherefore? For there follow other days
  And other lessons; other lips to praise
And to condemn. So let the past go by.
In truth we were not idlers, thou and I,
  Though oft we wandered in the woodland ways,
  And wronged the student's conscience by the gaze
We stole from books to fasten on the sky.
Some tasks we shunned, where many tasks were set,
  But never shunned each other. Was it well?
And much we learned we swiftly shall forget;
  But let no melancholy prophet tell
That ever pride or shame, or smiles or tears,
Shall dim the friendship of our college years.

                    KATHARINE LEE BATES.

If Life were a Banquet.

IF Life were a banquet, and Beauty were wine,
   And Being the cup to contain it,
What duty had man save at ease to recline,
   Drink deeply, and never disdain it?
If Life were a banquet, and Beauty were wine,
   And Being the cup to contain it!

If Life were a banquet, and Glory were wine,
   And Pain were the strong bowl that held it,
Would any man pause ere he quaffed, or repine
   At the cost, though his heart's blood had swelled it?
If Life were a banquet, and Glory were wine,
   And Pain were the strong bowl that held it!

If Life were a banquet, and Love were the wine,
   And pure lips alone touched the chalice,
What soul would refuse for a draught so divine,
   To purge itself wholly from malice?
But Life *is* a banquet, and Love *is* the wine,
   And pure lips alone touch the chalice!

JOSEPHINE A. CASS.

In the College Library.

TO L. E. W.

ALONE, absorbed, she sits and reads,
From heavy tomes of dingy brown,
The history of ancient deeds,
Of old beliefs, of worn-out creeds;
And, flooding all the open space,
The sun shines in upon the place,
Rests lightly on that fresh young face,
Revealing, in her simple grace,
    Elizabeth in cap and gown.

What though no lover may adore,
And marble heroes all look down
With cold eyes, changeless evermore,
At this sweet girl, a sophomore?
I know no picture half so fair
As she is, with her dark-brown hair,
Her earnest face, her gentle air.
May Heaven bless her, reading there,—
    Elizabeth, in cap and gown!

                  CORNELIA E. GREEN.

The Bachelor of Arts,
  December, 1895.

The Violinist.

BUT that one air for all that throng! And yet
    How variously the magic strain swept through
  Those thousand hearts! I saw young eyes, that knew
Only earth's fairest sights, grow dim and wet;
While eyes long fed on visions of regret,
    Beheld the rose of hope spring up from rue.
    For some, the night-wind in thy music blew;
For some, the spring's celestial clarinet!
And each heart knew its own: the poet heard,
    Ravished, the song his lips could never free;
The girl, her lover's swift, impassioned word;
The mother thought, "Oh little, buried face!"
    And one, through veil of doubt and agony,
Saw Christ, alone in the dim garden-place!

                MARGARET STEELE ANDERSON.
The Independent.

Mona Lisa.

A NGEL or sorceress! breathe me where lies
  Thy charm! Oh, the dark wonder of thy face,
  Where beauty and malignity embrace!
The covert joy within the shadow'd eyes,
The mirth upon the lips which knew no sighs,
  The brow whereon life's conflicts left no trace,
  The look inscrutable past time and space,
Bespeak a soul that knew not sacrifice!
Faithless and heartless, Mona Lisa, such
  Thou wert; and he who loved thee doth confess
Thy guilty soul by his fine, artist touch,—
  His genius still unerring,—yet not less
He loved thee madly, though thou gav'st not much
  Who gav'st of love all but its happiness.

ABBE CARTER GOODLOE.
The New England Magazine.

The Singer's Excuse.

I READ our sweetest singers' words,
   I hear the music of their voices;
The century's a cage of birds,
   The multiplying flock rejoices.
"Too many far," the critics scold;
   "Too many," the faint-hearted falter:
Remonstrance, haughty-browed and cold,
   The swelling chorus cannot alter.

What vibrant string forgets to ring
   When kindred sounds are near it throbbing?
Thou canst not scorn, Apollo, king!
   The lowliest reed thy breath sets sobbing.
The molten feeling in us lies,—
   The heart to word and rhyme must coin it.
Ah! who can hear the anthem rise
   Without a throat that aches to join it?

Oh! some may sing for all the years,
   And some for but the fleeting minute;
But singing keeps at bay our fears,
   And each and all have comfort in it.

Oh! some may sing for all mankind,
  And some for but a single hearer;
And one the greater praise may find,
  And one—to one at least—be dearer.

MARY RUSSELL BARTLETT.

The Century, "In Lighter Vein."
April, 1893.

Mutation.

I CAUGHT a snowflake in my hand,
      Six-pointed star,
God-fashioned still, and perfect planned,
      Though least and far.
With earthborn impulse swift I clasped it near,—
The crystal in my hand was changed a tear.

A dream upon a human heart
      Was waft to-day,
And fell soft-free, was clutched, to start
      In pain away.
A flitting thought in heaven gave it birth,
It came to be a human tear—on earth.

MARY HEFFERAN.

Trust.

MY beautiful life, with thy dome of blue,
   Thy wine of sunshine, thy calm of dew,
Thy bird song trilling the forest through,
Thy blush of morning and evening glow,
Thy joy of myriad lives that grow,
Of myriad blossoms that bud and blow,—
My beautiful life, I love thee so!
Sing sweet refrain in my heart again:
God is love! God is love! By his gifts I know
   God is love.

My desolate life, with thy sky of lead,
Thy wintry sunshine, thy bird song fled,
And only the snow-heaped graves of my dead!
Yet through thy darkness a glory glows,
And life is springing beneath thy snows,
And ever nearer the morning grows.
Sing, deep refrain, in my heart again:
God is love! God is love! In my grief I know
   God is love.

HELEN BARRETT MONTGOMERY.

The World's Sleep.

HASTE, cover yourself in the shrouded skies,
   Faint moon, with your broken ring;
And curious stars, bind fast your eyes
   With the clouds that the rain winds bring.
Deep, motionless night, with your mantle dark
   Of silence and shadow deep,
Bend closer while watching, the long hours mark,
   And let the old world sleep.

Whispering wind of the wandering feet,
   Steal back to the forest shade;
Break not the quiet, so still, so sweet,
   That over the world is laid:
For the world is so weary, so sad with woe,
   Wake it and it will weep;
Compassionate wind, breathe soft and go,
   And let the old world sleep.

SARAH CHAMBERLIN WEED.

Ode on the Planting of the First Class Tree.

LONG ago, the legends tell us,
   In a land across the seas,
Lived a people strong and warlike,
   And their gods were forest trees.

Each man loved his own, and watched it
   With a proud and anxious heart,
Tending it as if it truly
   Of his own life were a part.

If the gentle winds of heaven,
   Whisp'ring low, its leaflets stirred,
Then he listened most devoutly
   To the mystic, god-sent word.

If the terror of the lightning
   Scorched it with its fiery breath,
Then he paid it higher reverence,
   As a sign of his own death:

Said: "My stricken Mediator
   Shows me, by this sudden sign,
That my life and strength, so closely
   Joined to his, like his decline."

So of old they lived and worshiped,
　　Feeling that some subtle plan
Linked the life and growth in Nature
　　To the life and growth in man.

Centuries have bloomed and faded,
　　Nations, now forgotten, sleep,
And the agèd Past, in silence,
　　Hold their secrets buried deep.

Man has risen, life is broader,
　　Is a nobler, grander thing;
Sweeter now its lyric measures,
　　And its pæans louder ring.

Yet to us the Past has given
　　Myriad thoughts we call our own,
And we still are reaping harvests
　　From the seed that it has sown.

And we know, tho' half unconscious,
　　Still remains the old, old thought
Of our sympathy with Nature
　　Which their weird religion taught.

Still we feel that God is nearest
　In the ancient forest shade:
To the spirit of the Woodland,
　Man has ever homage paid.

Then blow, friendly winds of heaven,
　O'er the charge we leave you here;
And ye summer rains, fall gently,—
　Sunny skies, bend down to cheer!

And O Ruler of the storm-clouds,
　Master of the winds and sky,
We, thy children, crave thy sunshine,
　Losing which we droop and die.

May we change, like this our emblem,
　Earthy dross, to fairest life,
By thy aid gain strength and beauty
　From the elemental strife.

　　　　　　　　　CLARA A. JONES.

Ode to Wellesley.

[From Canto V.]

UPON thy altar, Wellesley, glows
    A living spark that ever burns,
    Fanned by each longing heart that yearns
For all the gifts that learning shows.
   .   .   .   .   .   .
Then mould each daughter strong and fair,
    With supple sinew, nerve, and power,
    With beauty as her rightful dower,
And pure as God's own thought of her;
Grant her the comprehensive mind
    That moves as planets in their arc,
    Whose all-embracing circles mark
The farthest ripple of the mind;
Yet leave her humble, gracious, kind,
    And artless as the wayside flower.
This is thy grand ideal of good:
    A truer heart, a clearer eye,—
    A proud, deep-bosomed race and high,
With less of passion in the blood,
And more and more of motherhood!

              ANNA ROBERTSON BROWN LINDSAY.

The Ideal.

BY the promise of noon's blue splendor in the
dawn's first silvery gleam,
By the song of the sea that compelleth the path of
the rock-cleaving stream,
I summon thee, recreant dreamer, to rise and follow
thy dream.

At the inmost core of thy being I am a burning
fire,
From thine own altar flame kindled, in the hour
when souls aspire;
For know that men's prayers shall be answered,
and guard thy spirit's desire.

That which thou would'st be thou must be, that
which thou shalt be thou art:
As the oak, astir in the acorn, the dull earth rend-
eth apart,
Lo, thou, the seed of thy longing, that breaketh
and waketh the heart!

Mine is the cry of the night wind, startling thy traitorous sleep;
Moaning I echo thy music, and e'en while thou boastest to reap
Alien harvests, my anger resounds from the vehement deep.

I am the solitude folding thy soul in a sudden embrace;
Faint waxes the voice of thy fellow, wan the light on his face;
Life is as cloud-drift about thee alone in shelterless space.

I am the drawn sword barring the lanes thy mutinous feet
Vainly covet for greenness. Loitering pace or fleet,
Thine is the crag-path chosen; on the crest shall rest be sweet.

I am thy strong consoler, when the desolate human pain
Darkens upon thee, the azure out-blotted by rush of the rain.
All that thou dost cherish may perish; still shall thy quest remain.

Call me thy foe in thy passion; claim me in peace
  for thy friend;
Yet bethink thee by lowland or upland, wherever
  thou willest to wend,
I am thine Angel of Judgment; mine eyes thou
  must meet in the end.

KATHARINE LEE BATES.

Shakespeare.

HE has been dead so many years!
  The record on his grave is dim,
And yet—the men one sees and hears,
  How dead they seem compared to him.

CHARLOTTE ROSE STANLEY.

George Birthington's Washday.

THERE was a famous washing day, its action near the Hub:
A Nation's raiment in the suds, a hero at the tub.
Then come, ye loyal patriots, and listen to my lay!
I'll sing of good George Birthington on this, his washing day.

"The time is come," said Birthington, "when wash we really must,
For, see our country's garments, how they're trampled in the dust;
And Liberty's bright tunic is so sadly soiled, I ween,
That nothing but a washing day will make it bright and clean."

The morning dawned, the washers came, the washing was begun;
The steam rose high, nor ceased to rise till cleanliness was won.
And now, though good George Birthington is gone to his repose,
The grateful country still recalls how well he washed her clothes.

FLORENCE E. HOMER.

The Lay of the Lost Hero.

I.

HOW sweet it was in by-gone times, upon a leisure day,
To take a novel from the shelf and while the hours away;
And with our kindly author-guide to wander hand in hand
Among the many winding paths of love's own fairy-land.
How sweet to toss the world aside, and in that freer air,
Forget that there existed aught but beauty anywhere;
To feel the cool, delicious wind blow on us fresh and strong,
And watch the troop of men and maids trip merrily along!

What matters if a cloud appeared in that serene blue sky?
It lasted but a moment's space, and then passed lightly by.

What matter if some thorns there were in paths
    true love must tread?
We knew that there were thornless flowers of happi-
    ness ahead.
Yea, though Sir Villain plot his worst, and steep
    himself in crime,
His efforts, it was safe to say, were but a waste of
    time;
For always in love's fairy-land of one thing we are
    sure,
Whatever woes the faithful pair of lovers may en-
    dure,
        Kind fate will let the hero win
        The beautiful young heroine.

II.

Now, sad to say, this all is changed. Our novel-
    reading hours
We can no longer spend among those paths be-
    strewn with flowers;
But, dragged into a wilderness, we soon have lost
    our way,
Entangled in that thicket dense, the Problem of
    the Day.

Our hero, gay and brave before, has vanished with
    a sigh,
Which is not strange when we perceive the heroine
    near by;
For how can this poor youth exist (e'en though he
    should prefer)
With qualities, both good and bad, monopolized by
    Her?

One grand, gigantic form alone comes slowly mov-
    ing on;
All others shrink to nothingness beside this Amazon.
What does she want with heroes, pray, when her
    determined plan
Consists in showing to the world the wickedness of
    man?
Yet e'en our friend the villain bold, must think it
    hardly fair
That he is forced to sin his sins with such an
    humble air.
Ah! hopeless is the task indeed, and pitiable the fate
Of him who dares attempt to write a novel up to date,—
        For with the modern heroine
        You *cannot* get a hero in.

CORNELIA E. GREEN.

Chap-Book,
    April 15, 1896.

Compensation.

SO long she has worn this mask of calm content,
　Through hours and days of never-ceasing care,
　　Learning with steady hope to lift and bear
　The bitter, weary burden of life's stent,
　She gives no sign of sorrow, nor the pent,
　　Choked anguish of an aching heart,—with rare
　　Sweet art concealing pain and all the wear
　And fret of disappointment, as one sent
　To show forth lasting patience. And the smile
　　That glorifies with constant light her face,
　　Though borrowed first to hide the scars of grief,
　Is now indeed her own;—for while
　　She gladdened others in the darksome place,
　　Her sad soul found, in smiling, self-relief.

MABEL A. CARPENTER.

The New England Magazine,
　October, 1896.

My Own.

BROWN heads and gold around my knee
    Dispute in eager play;
Sweet, childish voices in my ear
    Are sounding all the day;
Yet sometimes in a sudden hush
    I seem to hear a tone
Such as my little boy's had been,
    If I had kept my own.

And ofttimes when they come to me
    As evening hours grow long,
And beg me, winningly, to give
    A story or a song,
I see a pair of star-bright eyes
    Among the others shine,—
The eyes of him who ne'er hath heard
    Story or song of mine.

At night, I go my round and pause
    Each white-draped cot beside,
And note how flushed is this one's cheek,
    How that one's curls lie wide;

And to a corner tenantless
   My swift thoughts go apace;—
That would have been, if he had lived,
   My other darling's place.

The years go fast; my children soon
   Within the world of men
Will find their work, and venture forth
   Not to return again;
But there is one who cannot go,—
   I shall not be alone,—
The little one who did not live
   Will always be my own.

MARY WRIGHT PLUMMER.

The Century Magazine,
   March, 1882.

Four-o'clocks.

IT was that they loved the children,
　The children used to say,
　　For there was no doubt
　　That when school was out,
　At the same time every day,
　　Down by the wall,
　　Where the grass grew tall,
Under the hedge of the hollyhocks,
　　One by one,
　　At the touch of the sun,
There opened the four-o'clocks.

It was that they loved the children;—
　But the children have gone away,
　　And somebody goes
　　When nobody knows,
　At the same time every day,
　　To see by the wall,
　　Where the grass grows tall,
Under the hedge of the hollyhocks,
　　How, one by one,
　　At the touch of the sun,
Still open the four-o'clocks.

　　　　　　　　　LILLIAN B. QUIMBY.

In Memoriam: Helen A. Shafer.

OUR world had need of her, but God unrolled
   His larger plan, and without word or stir,
  Answering glad the Voice that cannot err,
She passed into the silence and His fold.
Soft, mellow sunshine filled the earth with gold
   The day she left it. We that dare aver
  We live in deeds, not hours, know life, in her,
Was nobly lived ere Psalmist's years were told.
Father, thy will be done! All things are good
   Thou sendest us, altho' we think them ill;
And what seems ill, Thy plan misunderstood.
We know she walks in brighter, happier ways
To-day than yesterday, so give Thee praise,
   And smile thro' tears that mourn our leader still.

                    MARTHA GAUSE MCCAULLEY.

All Hail to the College Beautiful!

ALL hail to the College Beautiful!
   All hail to the Wellesley blue!
All hail to the girls who are gath'ring pearls
   From the shells that are open to few:
From the shells upcast by the ebbing Past
   On the shores where, faithful and true,
An earnest band with the groping hand
Are seeking the jewels from under the sand;
And spreading abroad through the length of the land,
   The name of the Wellesley blue.

CHORUS.

   All hail to the College Beautiful!
   All hail to the royal throne,
   Whence her heart within her burning,
   Silver-voicèd, far-eyed Learning
   Looks upon her own.

All hail to the College Beautiful!
   All hail to the brave and bright!
She has taken her place in the swift-sandaled race,
   Where the strong man smiles in his might.

Oh! shining arise the lights in her eyes,
And her hands are hot for the prize.
Now fast and far let the race be tried!
She runs in her weakness and he in his pride;
But run as they will, they will run side by side,
   And share in the victor's right.

All hail to the College Beautiful!
   All hail to the sacred walls,
Where, sinking away in the shadowy gray,
   Aye, the sun's last radiance falls;
Where first on the lake the day beams awake,
And the Spring's white manacles break.
But flushed in waking or pale in rest,
With leaves on her hair or with snows on her breast,
Forever the fairest, and noblest, and best,
   All hail to her sacred walls.

KATHARINE LEE BATES.

The Angelus.

THE glowing evening light is in the west;
    The day is almost done. Across the land
Comes faint and sweet the Angelus' command,
"Give God due praise and get thee to thy rest."

Two figures standing with heads bowed in prayer,
    A man and woman, each in peasant dress;
    She with clasped hands which 'gainst her bosom press,
He with his head bared to the evening air.

So still they stand! God's presence sure is near,
    God's comfort calmeth now the toil-worn heart,
    Which stealeth from earth's weariness apart,
And seeketh Him, well knowing He will hear.

Two peasants and the sunset's golden light,
    A church tower, from which faint and sweet outrings
    The Angelus: "Put by all earthly things;
Turn to thy rest. The dear God sendeth night."

                    JOSEPHINE P. SIMRALL.

The Heart's Home.

AS swift in the dying west
  The bird flies home to her nest,
My heart thus turneth to thee,
To thee, sweet love, to thee.

The bird, in her downy nest,
My heart in thee, finds rest.
Though branches rock and sway
The bird sits safe alway.

KATHARINE MORDANTT QUINT.

Waking-Time.

ON the cradling boughs
  Cuddled limbs arouse;
Bonny babes get up from curtained beds below:
  Pinafores of green,
  Caps of gayest sheen,
They'll wear for summer frolics to and fro.

ADA MAY KRECKER.

Lalia.

MY Lalia breathes love on the roses,
   But I,—though a rose is a queen,—
I have whispered to her that the rarest of buds
   By her rose-lips would wither unseen.

In the depths of the violet meadows
   Kneels Lalia, a votaress fair,
And the truth in her heart holds the blue in
      her eyes
   Fadeless, resistless, and rare.

My Lalia prays over the lilies,
   But I,—though the lilies' true knight,—
I have said to my love that I find her pure soul
   Than the exquisite lilies more white.

FLORENCE ANNETTE WING.

A Song of Praise.
(In Memory of Phillips Brooks.)

I.

O PERFECT God, who sendest of Thy grace
Each perfect gift to us Thy children here,
Sunshine and showers, the summer's radiant face
And spring's divinest message, starry sphere,
And dewy rose, and music, and the near
Sweet human joys of kindred and of home,
Love, hope, endeavor, faith, and noble cheer
Of prophet souls that down thy pathways come,
Proving our earth thy feast, our skies thy temple-
    dome,—

II.

We praise thee; we acknowledge thee, O Lord,
Our angel's Angel and our Gift Supreme.
And now, if ever earnestness implored
Thy guidance, deign to lend it, for the theme
That lifts our hearts is in Thy heart, we deem,
Held precious. Wherefore touch with cleansing
    fire,
Pure from Thine altar's height, these lips, that
    seem
Presumptuous, yet cannot choose; inspire
This tongue with truth, sustain this consecrate desire!

III.

We praise Thee, then, that in these latter days,
When our dark earth is slowly turning still
Into Thy steadfast light, but mortal ways
Are tangled yet with myriad skeins of ill,
Thy love has sent a *man*, who should fulfill
Again the ancient oracles, and stand
A tower of adamant on a storm-swept hill,
A great rock's shadow in a weary land,
Health to the sick, deliverance to the blind and banned.

IV.

Let no man fear our Lord is honored less,
When his foreshadowing paints his servant too.
Nay, rather hold in awe the clear impress
Of Christ's own pattern on a spirit new,
A spirit to its Master sternly true.
The Christ in him so lived and strove and wrought,
So wondrously through all his being grew,
That in his eyes we read Christ's very thought,
And in his smile a hint of Christ's own smile we caught.

V.

Among his kind he dwelt in simple wise,
Choosing and claiming as his dearest right
The common lot, the universal ties,
The plain experiences that flashed with light,
Transfigured, in his essence-piercing sight;
Keeping his golden dower of privilege,
Birth, riches, learning, genius, duly bright
With shining use, yet plucking still the pledge
Of loftiest joy along the highway's dusty edge.

VI.

Yea, common paths he loved and common men;
All human souls his brothers; not in creed
Alone, but passionately proven, when
Each eager word was sealed with eager deed.
The great heart's torrent, struggling to be freed
And rush in shoreless blessing everywhere—
The deep heart's tenderness, that fain would bleed
His life out, drop by drop, if he might share
And heal our woes—who can forget, and who declare!

VII.

So close his walk with God, so thin the veil
That from encompassing eternity
Still held his vision, that his every tale
Of lands celestial was a thing to see,
Stamped with the proof-mark of reality.
So free he dwelt in God's high fatherhood,
Our faith through his grew son-like, glad, and
    free;
Conscious of God in all the world of good,
Trusting to God to spare or slay us, as He would.

VIII.

A kingly presence, robed in white array,
As angels use; a rapt, uplifted face,
And holy eyes that greet the heavenly day
Afar beyond our walls of time and space;
Grand, searching eyes that earthward turn apace,
And brooding o'er the multitudinous throng
That surges to the very altar-place,
  Drink deep its inspiration; lips that long
Have charged themselves with noblest meanings,
    victor-strong.

IX.

A rapid, reverent, self-unconscious voice, '
Making his people's every prayer his own;
How often shall their dreaming ears rejoice
To trace the old belovèd undertone
Through the great ritual they with him have known!
How often shall their souls exult again,
Hearing that voice, to glorious music grown,
Pealing out ecstasy to heart and brain,
Pouring out faith sublime and hope's immortal rain!

X.

Earth wails her "Nevermore!" against the sound;
Earth strives to shut the vision from our sight
And leave one master-memory: life is crowned
With death; with funeral pomp his couch is dight;
Majestic peace sleeps on his eyelids white;
His country's banners watch her patriot's bed;
His country's guards wait in the solemn light;
While slow, exalted, with bewildered tread,
Passes the host unknown, and now unshepherded.

XI.

Unshepherded? And here our Galahad lies
Stricken, beneath the lilies of his dreams?
Ah, no! in golden fields of Paradise
He laughs with God beside the living streams.
Almost we catch the swift, supernal gleams
His garments leave in passing; almost know,
By sense more sure than that which surest
    seems,
The benedictions from his throne that flow,
The throne God shares with him who overcame below.

XII.

He loved his people; in his Christ-like love
He gave himself to us: that gift no power
In earth or heaven or unguessed heights above
Can take away: himself; not the frail dower
Of mortal grace, the splendor of an hour;
But that great character, that vital truth,
Which entered into us, and flushed to flower
Each skyward bud, each struggling aim un-
    couth;
Claiming for God the King our holy land of youth.

XIII.

O ye his kindred, ye his chosen peers,
Robed in the purple of his heart's conferring,
We bow before your grief: the buried years
Still in your faith's divinest triumph stirring
Exquisite memories, poignantly recurring!
But we, the people, who in spirit met,
In spirit only, loved him,—nought deterring,
Grow in his angel-growth but richer yet,—
Our souls his monument, when centuries forget!

MARION PELTON GUILD.

Sunset.

THE golden glory quivers on the lake,
    A robin's vesper note sounds clear and true;
Beyond the far hill line one long pale cloud
    Lies, like a thought of God, across the blue.

MARY HOLLANDS McLEAN.

"At Wellesley."

Sleeplessness.

WITHIN,—
 There are four low walls, and one overhead,—
White, white walls,—and a small white bed,
Where I lie with mine eyes wide-opened,
 For Sleep is sitting without.

Within,—
There's a wide-waked soul that sighs and sings
Restless thoughts of restful things;
There are dreams that beat on the walls with their
 wings,
 For Sleep is sitting without.

Within,—
There's a wistful, wide-eyed wakefulness,
Never to be stilled unless
Sleep cometh in at the door to bless,—
 And Sleep is sitting without.

FLORENCE CONVERSE.

My College Room.
(A Farewell.)

A LOVING look I give around the room:
   Here Beatrice Cenci's earnest gaze
  For simple justice pleads with me; a haze
Enshadows mournful Sappho in its gloom.

And near a sunny Rome is Effie Deans,
   Some photographs are o'er my laden shelves;
   And wondrous wealth is here for one who delves.
Above my desk a singing cherub leans.

Ah! hov'ring o'er the pictures in the shade
   I see the wraith of days when pain was here,
   And troublous times that only prayer could cheer,
And doubts and fears and struggles that I had.

But in the golden shimmer that the lake
   Reflects upon the wall I see my joys.
   One moment are the sad and glad in poise;
But glad outweighs,—the lights and shadows break!

                MABEL WING CASTLE.

Culture.

THEY stood and talked together at the hour
  Of night when constellations brightest shine;
The cloud-drifts, rent and torn, wind-blown, were
    clasped
  With borrowed silver, curved in molten line.

In thoughtful tone, from heart sincere and tried,—
  One heard 'twas friend to friend,—the first one
    spoke.
The solemn glory of the full-orbed moon
  Serene from out the parting cloud-bank broke.

"How great a power has written yonder law,
  That moves resistless on in every star!
Sublime the joy to man, who dares to know
  The system far beyond his make or mar.

"The course of every planet, of each moon,
  As surely shaped yon shaft of radiant cloud
As the light wind-puff driving it so swift
  Across the rounded disc of Cynthia proud.

"Oh! what were life if thou, sublimest scroll,
　Were a black-letter page to my dull, darkened soul?"
His friend but waited till the flash and fire died
From out the air, and quietly replied:—

"With you I feel that not to know is death;
　From there our sympathies seem to divide.
While you exult in knowledge, science broad,
　I lose the science in the stillness wide.

"Forget, you know! we cannot see the all,
　Save as we fail to think of knowledge, law.
Rest conscious in resource of latent power,
　And give yourself thus to a higher awe.

"Sublime the sense of ordered, noted life;
　But lost within the rapturous, swelling whole.
Divine the sense of law and spirit fused,
　Not mind, not heart, but all-embracing soul!"

　　　　　　　　　ANNA ESTELLE WOLFSON.

Dolores.

THROUGH the streets of fair Sevilla
    Roams the happy Gypsy maid;
Blithe she singeth, lithe she danceth,
    'Neath the orange's welcome shade.
Care she feels not, sorrow knows not,
    Free as air, as ocean's foam,
'Neath the blue arch of the heavens
    Is the dark-eyed maiden's home.
O Dolores, Gypsy maiden,
    Singing to thy light guitar,
O Dolores, Gypsy maiden,
    O Dolores, Zingara!

Oleanders pink with clusters,
    Sage green of the olive tree,
Waving branches, flitting sunlight,
    Make a picture fit for thee.
Slender ankles, brown and shapely,
    Wondrous tresses, dark as night,
Graceful form in every movement,
    Scarlet bodice, skirt of white.

O Dolores, Gypsy maiden,
   Dancing to the light guitar,
O Dolores, Gypsy maiden,
   O Dolores, Zingara!

Now she comes with soft voice pleading.
   List! "Por l'amor de Dios;"
Ah, Senora, how bewitching,
   And a glittering coin we toss.
Then again for us she danceth,
   Throwing high her lovely arms,
Fluttering like a bird its plumage,
   Giving glimpses of her charms.
O Dolores, Gypsy maiden,
   Dancing to the light guitar,
O Dolores, Gypsy maiden,
   O Dolores, Zingara!

Ah, Sevilla, we must leave thee,
"Adios," to sunny Spain;
Daughter of the dark Gitanos,
   We may see thee ne'er again.

Pepper trees with scarlet berries,
  Cactus hedges, olives green,
Just between thy twinkling shadows
  Is the little Gypsy seen.
Ah, Dolores, thou art weeping,
  Weeping by thy light guitar;
"Adios," O Gypsy maiden,
  O Dolores, Zingara!

JOSEPHA VIRGINIA SWEETSER.

The Canterbury Tales.

I LOVE to read the tales in merry rhyme
  Of bold adventure or of jollity,
Wherewith those olden pilgrims passed their time;
And often have I wished that I might see
Upon their way that very company—
The dainty nun, the knight with burnished lance,
Most dear—the poet's gentle countenance.

ADA MAY KRECKER.

In Arcadie.

HOW swift the days fled, one by one,
    In Arcadie, in Arcadie!
And when we thought them just begun,
(Those happy days!) the last was gone,
And we no more might linger on
    In Arcadie.

Fair days, descending from the blue
    On Arcadie, on Arcadie!
Some queens, and crowned with diamond dew,
By gleaming robes of sunlight gold
Enwrapt, in many a wind-swayed fold,
    In Arcadie.

And some were Quakers clad in gray
    In Arcadie, in Arcadie;
And passed serenely on their way,
Silent, as pondering some sweet thought,
From Goethe or from Homer brought,
    In Arcadie.

Some days were angels, white and tall,
    In Arcadie, in Arcadie,
Who led us to confessional,
There bade us of our sins repent,
And softly blessed us ere we went,
    In Arcadie.

And oreads some, lithe-limbed and strong,
    In Arcadie, in Arcadie—
With laughing eyes, forever young;
Our guides were they to mount and glen,
Green-robed, like Robin's merry men,
    In Arcadie.

And lo! we stood on many a height
    In Arcadie, in Arcadie;
The stream that lay in curves of light
Before our feet, through yon blue rift
Rolled seaward, silently and swift,
    Through Arcadie.

That mountain-barrier, faint and far
    Round Arcadie, round Arcadie,

It shuts us in with moon and star,
With sunset splendors, dawn delights,
And all the train of silver nights,
　　In Arcadie!

　．　．　．　．　．　．　．　．　．　．

And some there met who ne'er will part,
　　In Arcadie, in Arcadie;
For lands divide not heart from heart,
And friends are friends on sea or shore,
Although they wander nevermore
　　In Arcadie!

　　　　　　　　　　JOSEPHINE A. CASS.
Boston Transcript.

Seaward.

IN the heart of the hills a lingering stream
  Goes songfully on to meet the sea;
In the heart of the hills, enthralled in a dream,
  My life waits wistfully.

I kneel me down where the waters pass,
  'Mid purpling flags and lilies of white;
I bury my face in the long sedge-grass
  That the waves kiss in their flight.

I whisper down through the water's sheen,
  "Oh, stream, thou art brave to seek the sea;
'Mid the sin and the shame that wait between,
  Thou wilt lose thy purity.

"I dreamed a dream of the hidden years,
  And my heart is songless, my lips are dumb,
My eyes are wet with the whole world's tears,
  For the sin and the shame to come."

The stream made answer in glimmer and glow:
"In spite of purity, lost or won,
The stately ships pass to and fro,
  And the world's work must be done.

"Beyond the pain, and beyond the mist
  There waits forever the vast of the sea,
And the voice of the hoar Evangelist
  Thunders, 'Eternity.'"

There with my face in the cool sedge-grass,
  I heard the murmur of waters that flee,
I caught the flutter of wings that pass,
  And my soul longed to be free.

My heart grew eager to bear and know
  The toil, the pain, the shame and the strife,
That rise and gain in the ebb and flow
  Of the restless waters of life.

Then, where the hills encircled me,
  Outpouring from water, and air, and sod,
I caught the sweep of the measureless sea
  Of the infinite spirit of God.

In the heart of the hills, a lingering stream
  Goes silently on to meet the sea;
In the heart of the hills, enthralled in a dream,
  My life waits wistfully.

ADA S. WOOLFOLK.

The Empty Nest.

A NEST in the tree top swinging;
An oriole gayly singing:
Sweet and low, sweet and low,
To and fro, to and fro.
Sing, quivering breast!
Swing, birdlings at rest
In your cradle the green leaves under!
Warm little nest,
Sheltered and blest,
Will it always be so, I wonder?

The wind in the tree tops sighing,
In the leafless branches dying!
Sad and slow, to and fro,
Swings a nest filled with snow.
Ah me! nevermore
Shall a bright wing soar
From that nest 'neath the leaves suspended.
Empty and bare
It hangeth there,
The wraith of a summer ended.

HELEN BARRETT MONTGOMERY.

Song.

WHEN other hearts are light and gay,
    And life holds carnival in May,—.
        Some gladness borrow.
O, not upon that joy intrude
Thy grief, but seek in solitude
        A balm for sorrow.

When other heads are bowed, and grief
Doth settle with the falling leaf,—
        Make no complaining.
O, do not bring thy burden there
To add to woe, but hide thy care,
        All sign disdaining.

                CHARLOTTE ROSE STANLEY.

My College Girl.
(A Father's Soliloquy.)

SHE is skilled in Mathematics,
    And knows more of Hydrostatics
Than I learned in all my plodding years at Yale.
    She performs experiments
    With the divers elements,
That would make her little brother's cheek turn pale.

    She can French and German speak,
    And can write in Ancient Greek,
Getting all the various accents quite correct.
    Though she deals hard blows at Russians
    In historical discussions,
In her logic not a flaw can I detect.

    She, altho' 'tis not her habit,
    Can dissect a good sized rabbit,
Giving you the name of each and every bone.
    Much she knows of plant and tree,
    On the land or in the sea,
Slighting not meanwhile the all-important stone.

    Like a statue can she pose,
    And interpret learnèd prose
In a way that makes my pulses wildly beat.
    She has studied poetry,—lyric,
    Epic also, and satiric,—
Till her diction and her style are quite complete.

    She has studied *me*,—the sinner!—
    And can cook as good a dinner
As a hungry man would ever wish to spy.
    And I challenge the world over,
    If two folk they can discover
Quite so happy as my college girl and I.

                  ALICE WELCH KELLOGG.

SLENDER, brown-haired Josephine,
    With the eyes of blue!
  I'm no gifted cavalier,
  I've not fame, nor wealth, 'tis clear;
  But I love you oceans, dear!
    Won't that do?

Ode.

(Written for the Opening of the Woman's Building, World's Fair, 1893.)

FROM the lovely land of Alhambra and out from the mists of the years,
Let us summon a presence before us, as spirits are summoned by Seers.
Behold, a woman is standing, the glitter of gems in her hands,
With far-gazing eyes that are turned toward the rim of invisible lands.
Behold her, royally bending to heed a stranger's appeal,
With gift of grace and of godspeed, Isabella, the Queen of Castile.
Let us join to man's glory the woman's, the glory of faith and of deed
That cheered the brave mariner on in the day of his desperate need.
He, sailing, and sailing, and into the sunset seas,
Little dreamed of the land that he sailed to, the sage and the sad Genoese.

She, dreaming, and dreaming, and dreaming apart in
　her palace of Spain,
Little dreamed of the future awaiting that land of
　the Western Main;
The future, a plant of God's garden, unfolding in
　beauty supreme
To blossom into the splendor of this White City of
　Dream!
Not as Queen but as woman, we hail Isabella, and
　crown her to-day
In these halls that women have built and illumined
　with costly array.
Here, gravely let us be grateful, as heirs of a generous
　past,
For the pleasure, and powers, and duties fallen to
　woman at last.
They have yielded to her their kingdoms, science,
　and letters, and art,
And still she controls, undisputed, the realm of the
　home and the heart.

　　　　　　　　　　　　FLORENCE WILKINSON.
The Graphic,
　May 13, 1893.

Barriers.

HERE'S a leaf here,
There's a sky there,
  With space between;
Here's a bird here,
There's a nest there,
  With time between;
Here's a rose here,
There's a bud there,
  With life between;
Here's a grave here,
There's a child there,
  With death between;
Here's a smile here,
There's a smile there,
  With love between;
Here's a heart here,
There's a God there,
  And naught between.

HELEN WORTHINGTON ROGERS.

Journal of Education,
  Jan. 28, 1892.

Love Song.

DREAMS by day and thoughts by night
   Breathe of thee,
   Clouds in sky and waves in sea,
Springing grass and swallow's flight.

With thy voice was music born
   On the earth,
   Pipes Pandean, cymbals' mirth,
Trumpet-clang, and bugle-horn!

Beautiful the world and strong
   From thy face,
   Flushed with youth and free with grace,
That to gods of old belong.

Life is measured by the beat
   Of thy heart;
   Time began and shall depart
With the passing of thy feet.

                LILLIAN CORBETT BARNES.

Knowledge.

LIKE the dream of a drowsy flower,
    Fragrant and fleet;
Like the hope in the heart of a pansy,
    Dusky and sweet;
Like the passion of crimson roses
    Flung at one's feet:
Deep as the thoughts, beloved,
    I cannot say;
Dear as the faith in each other
    We lost, one day;
Strong as when souls forsaken
    Know no dismay:
Dear love, though I cannot tell you,
    All love can be,
Sometime—God willing—you shall, love,
    Try it and see.

Like the struggle of souls that are sleepless,
    Yearning for sleep;
Like the torture of eyes tear-laden,
    Forbidden to weep;
Like the ache of dumb lips that must ever
    In silence keep:

Like the pride of the lie, beloved,
    Though no one believes;
Like the laughter of eyes lest they show you
    A heart that grieves;
Like a voice seeking always an answer
    It never receives,—
Dear love, though I cannot tell you
    All pain can be,
From closer knowledge, I pray, love,
    God keep you free.

                LILLIAN B. QUIMBY.

Alone.

"NEVER alone again,"
    A strong arm held me fast;
Heart upon heart we crushed
    The loneness of the past.

Loosened the tender clasp,
    As love to darkness fled.
"Never alone before,"
    From out the void, I said.

                MAUD THOMPSON.

The Divine Right of Kings.

THE right divine! What king that hath it not?
　The right to look through all his realm and see
What fever courses in the people's veins,
And lay thereon the balm of kingly hands;
To turn aside the treasonable blade,
And make a friend of him who carries it;
To bind up public wounds; to put away
The screens wherewith men hide accusing truth,
And speak grave words when these befit the time;
To sow the land so full of happiness,
Of peace and justice, love and courtesy,
That ships bound seaward unto fabled shores
Shall never tempt his people otherwhere:
Such right divine as this hath every king.

MARY WRIGHT PLUMMER.

The Atlantic Monthly,
　May, 1882.

Omar Khayyám.

THOU great philosopher! to whom belong
  The laurels that a genius' brow entwine,
  Thy poet's mantle thou didst stain with wine,
Drowning thy bitter sadness in a song.
Through seven centuries, still clear and strong,
  Is sounding in our ears thy every line,
  Whilst thou, the singer, long since didst resign
This tangled earthly maze of right and wrong.
Somewhere, it may be, in that land unknown,
Where present, past, and future are made one,
  Thy hopeless vision of fulfilled desire
Is something nearer than a vision grown,
  And the deep shadow of a soul on fire,
Lost in the piercing brightness of the Sun.

                      CORNELIA E. GREEN.

April.

AFTER the month of the double face,
After St. Valentine's days of grace,
  After the blast of the trump of March,
With a smile and a tear, with a tear and a smile,
And a heart half winter's all the while,
  Here's the shy little month with her glances arch,
Here's the brave little month of folly!

    Rain, rain, with the sun between!
    Sun, sun, through the raindrop's sheen!
    Sing, two leaves in a sheath of green
      For the sweet little month of folly.

Before the simple troth of May,
Before the June in her bride's array,
  Before the splendor of harvest gold,
With a tear and a smile, with a smile and a tear,
And a heart that's pledged to the whole of the year,
  Here's the month of promise come out of the cold;
Here's the wise little month of folly!

Rain, rain, with the sun between!
Sun, sun, through the raindrop's sheen!
Sing, two leaves in a sheath of green
For the sweet little month of folly.

MARY RUSSELL BARTLETT.

The Independent,
  April, 1893.

A Picture.

A SUNSET of gold on the tree tops is gleaming,
  A glimmering sheen on the water's calm breast,
A boat, as it glides through sunset clear splendor,
  Bears Beauty and Gladness away to the west.

While eyes tell to eyes the sweet secret of loving,
  Blue eyes to brown, and brown eyes to blue,
Till deep in the heart of each, as they're drifting,
  There settles a glow like the sunset's rich hue.

Out of the glow; mid the shadows that gather
  Along the lone shore; in a maze of despair,
The soul of another, with loving and longing,
  Turns backward to night, to toil, and to prayer.

ALMA E. BEALE.

Idolatry.

ENSHRINED on high, in my soul's holy place,
   I made a god, what others called mere clay:
  I brought my all, and knelt there night and day,
With incense of pure love, and lifted face
Wet with hot tears; while in the altar space
   Honor, and fame, and pride I cast away.
  With outstretched, straining arms I strove to pray,
"O hear me, hear me; let my gifts find grace."

The dull eyes saw, unmoved; no answer came
   From the mute lips; but echo's mocking moan
  At last I knew; mine, only mine the blame:
Mere stone and wood; the folly, the dark shame!
   My punishment is on me; I have grown
   Like what I worshiped, senseless, soulless stone.

                          KENT DUNLAP HÄGLER.

A Hobby.

THERE is a sprightly maiden
   We all know very well,
Who rides a prancing hobby
   Upon which she loves to dwell.
This hobby is not learning,
   Though in that she does excel,
Nor yet the rights of woman,
   Which she upholds so well.

For dress reform she's striving,
   And more eloquent is she
Than any Daniel Webster
   Or a Henry Clay could be.
If her dress should be constricting
   To her super-human breath,
She would cry with Patrick Henry,
"Give me liberty, or death."

                    MABEL W. WHITE.

"Agnus Dei."

(Written on hearing a boys' choir sing Handel's Hallelujah Chorus.)

ROWS of earnest boyish faces
    Were before me, while the strain
Of a wondrous, glorious anthem
    Soared aloft, as if to gain
Entrance at the pearly portals
    Of the city paved with gold,
And the fresh, sweet, boyish voices,
    Sang once more the prayer of old.

"Lamb of God have mercy on us,
    Grant, O grant to us Thy peace!"
Agnus Dei, give them answer;
    May their praises never cease!
Then the victor's song of triumph;
    Loud the grand, sweet chorus rings,
"Hallelujah, hallelujah!
    Lord of lords, and King of kings."

And the boys were all so earnest,
    Sang with all their soul and might,
Still so young and unacquainted
    With the world's cold, weary night.

Can it be, I thought, and shuddered,
　That the boyish voices sweet
E'er shall speak, in words unholy,
　Things less grand, less pure, repeat?

Ah! there lies stretched out before them
　Life with all its various ways;
All will not be hallelujahs,
　All will not be songs of praise.
But the Lamb of God, who taketh
　From the world the stains of sin,
Ever liveth, never changeth:
　May He keep them pure within.

And my heart this prayer would offer:
　Thou great Shepherd of Thy sheep,
May these boys all know and love Thee,
　All Thy blessèd precepts keep.
Consecrate, dear Lord, and guard them,
　May their praises never cease:
"Lamb of God, have mercy on them;
　Grant, O grant to them Thy peace."

　　　　　　Josepha Virginia Sweetser.
The Watchman.

Country Children.

LITTLE fresh violets,
   Born in the wildwood,
Sweetly illustrating
   Innocent childhood!
Shy as an antelope
   Brown as a berry,
Free as the mountain air,
   Romping and merry.

Blue eyes and hazel eyes
   Peep from the hedges,
Shaded by sunbonnets
   Frayed at the edges;
Up in the apple tree,
   Heedless of danger,
Manhood in embryo
   Stares at the stranger.

Under the orchard trees
   Seeking for cherries,
Out in the meadow lands
   Hunting for berries;

Now in the clover fields,
   Tramping down grasses,
No voice to hinder them,
   Dear lads and lasses!

Little fresh violets,
   Born in the wildwood!
Oh that all little ones
   Had such a childhood!
God's blue spread over them,
   God's green beneath them,—
No sweeter heritage
   Could we bequeath them!

            MARY ALLISON BINGHAM.

Wellesley Democracy.

"WHY waste your time on him?" I said;
   "The man is silly, stupid, flat."
Rebelliously she shook her head,—
   "A man's a man for a' that."

            S.

Twilight on the Hills.

WARM and still, as if in dreaming,
  Lies the valley, green and low;
Trailing clouds above are gleaming
  In the sunset afterglow.

Changing, shifting, and dissolving,
  Paling in the purple west,
Man from toil and care absolving,
  See, they fold the world to rest.

Never yet in song or story,
  Though with color richly dight,
Has the poet caught the glory
  Of that amethystine light;

Shades too rare for pen of mortals,
  Tints of many a precious gem,
Like the stones beneath the portals
  Of the new Jerusalem.

For in opalescent splendor
   On the sunlit slopes are set
Hues of jacinth, pure and tender,
   Chrysoprase and violet.

And a strangely solemn gladness
   Steals across us from the steep,
Full of awe, and touched with sadness,—
   Longings infinite and deep.

Not as when on cloud-capped Sinai
   Lurid lightnings lit the gloom;
But as when the fair Shechinah
   Filled the aloe-scented room.

Such mute moods of nature win us
   To the holy calm of prayer;
And the yearning spirit in us,
   Cleansèd of its dark despair,

Rises far above terrestrial
   Moil and soul-corroding care,
And on wings of hope celestial
   Breathes a finer, freer air.

Twilight on the Hills.

WARM and still, as if in dreaming,
   Lies the valley, green and low;
Trailing clouds above are gleaming
   In the sunset afterglow.

Changing, shifting, and dissolving,
   Paling in the purple west,
Man from toil and care absolving,
   See, they fold the world to rest.

Never yet in song or story,
   Though with color richly dight,
Has the poet caught the glory
   Of that amethystine light;

Shades too rare for pen of mortals,
   Tints of many a precious gem,
Like the stones beneath the portals
   Of the new Jerusalem.

For in opalescent splendor
  On the sunlit slopes are set
Hues of jacinth, pure and tender,
  Chrysoprase and violet.

And a strangely solemn gladness
  Steals across us from the steep,
Full of awe, and touched with sadness,—
  Longings infinite and deep.

Not as when on cloud-capped Sinai
  Lurid lightnings lit the gloom;
But as when the fair Shechinah
  Filled the aloe-scented room.

Such mute moods of nature win us
  To the holy calm of prayer;
And the yearning spirit in us,
  Cleansèd of its dark despair,

Rises far above terrestrial
  Moil and soul-corroding care,
And on wings of hope celestial
  Breathes a finer, freer air.

Heaven seems so close above us,
   Earthly clamors softly cease;
In our hearts a gentle love is,
   Silence deep, and utter peace.

What are we that we should sigh at
   Aught that mars our joy to-day?
All unrest is hushed in quiet,
   Clamant passion dies away;

And our souls, so long by labor,
   Sin, and sore temptation tried,
Seem to stand at last on Tabor,
   Radiant and glorified!

              ANNA ROBERTSON BROWN LINDSAY.

Ode to Ninety-Six.

[Aspiration speaks on Truth.]

O WHITE soul, know thou well this one first truth,
That knowledge cannot compass nor endure,
That certainty conceals, none can be sure,
Yet in each one soul's limit the thread of Truth
Runs evermore, and links the good to good.
Scan close what then thou hast of knowledge won
Within the light of Truth. Search deep thine own
True ideal self, and in that self alone
Work out thy life's activity, and in the world
Where now thou goest know it all is part.
The world exists for thee; build thou thy world
According to the best thou canst discern;
Then shalt thou ever live, forever turn,
My star set close above, my lamp before thee,
To greet the new experience joyfully;
Till, all complete, the gray veil drawn away,
In the clear light of thine own heart
Truth stands revealed alway.

MARY HEFFERAN.

Tree-day Poem, 1896.

Compensation.

A SUMMER'S eve, a moonlit sky,
  A sea, soft water's purl,
A tiny boat, and two spoon-oars,
  A pretty Wellesley girl.

I watched her face; methought it glowed
  With trust and sweet content.
I paused, and resting both my oars,
  On tend'rest theme was bent,

When lo! she, grasping at those oars
  This scornful speech did throw:
"I cannot stand it any more;
  I'll show you how to row!

Like this—see there—you strike out so—
  Like that—'tis new to you?
'When did I learn?' O, long ago;
  I'm on a Wellesley Crew!"

I sat in silence meekly by,
  And swallowed all my pride,
While ev'ry pretty, tender word
  Was straightway petrified.

They ne'er were spoken, and I fear
They ne'er may spoken be;
But I can row the Wellesley stroke,
So what is that to me?

ALICE WELCH KELLOGG.

When the Mist Came up from the Marsh.

WHEN the mist came up from the marsh last night,
The moon hung low in the fading light
  Her golden bow in the western sky;
  A glow remained where the sunsets die,
When the mist came up from the marsh.

When the mist came up from the marsh last night,
The tangled reeds from the mantle white
  Stared out like thoughts thro' the mist of years,
  And the evening wind had a sound of tears,
When the mist came up from the marsh.

SARAH CHAMBERLIN WEED.

A Carol.

[Standard of the Cross.]

O'ER the silent meadows,
    O'er the sleeping town,
O'er the murmuring forest
    Pours a radiance down:
'Tis a starry splendor
    Glorifying night;
Shepherds, kings, and sages
    Wonder at the sight.

See, O kings and shepherds,
    Magi from afar,
Cradled in a manger
    Israel's Morning Star!
And through parted heavens
    Lo! the angelic throng
Voice their adoration
    In triumphant song.

O'er the silent meadows
    Floats the joyful strain;
O'er the murmuring forest
    List! it comes again:

"Glory in the highest!"
　Hark! O sleeping town;
"Peace, good will"—the blessing
　Still to earth comes down.

Still the starry wonder
　Of that long-past night
Gleams adown the ages,
　Filling all with light;
And all Nature, joining,
　Swells the anthem still,—
"Glory in the highest;
　On earth, peace, good will."

　　　　HARRIOT BREWER STERLING.

The Old Year.

"GOOD-BY," we say, but never part,
　Such tried, old friends as you and I!
In you, Old Year, I found my heart;
　In you I learned to live or die.

In you I learned to pity sin,
　In you to suffer and be strong;
In you to seek the peace within,
　To love the right and hate the wrong.

　　　　NANCY K. FOSTER.

Boo! Hoo!
[A Wellesley Glee.]

BOO! hoo! Mamma, take me home;
   Ev'rybody here's so hard on me.
Oh! oh! why did I from you roam,
   To take up my abode in Wellesley?
Boo! hoo! they fill up all my day
   With English, Greek and Latin, Math. and Gym.
Oh! oh! and then they kindly say,
"Plenty time to *spatziergehen* in."
Boo! hoo! Boo! hoo! Boo! hoo!

Boo! hoo! they say I must expand
   To meet the broader needs of woman kind.
Oh! oh! I think I'm fat enough
   To satisfy the most ambitious mind.
Boo! hoo! they make me dust and sweep
   A great big gloomy room, called P. L. R.
Oh! oh! they make me go to sleep
   No matter how unlearned my lessons are.
Boo! hoo! Boo! hoo! Boo! hoo!

Boo! hoo! I miss my dolly so!
   Won't you send her on, Ma? That's a dear.

Oh! oh! 'twould comfort me, I know,
  And then when I'm alone I'd have no fear.
Boo! hoo! I 'most forgot to say
  There are some dreadful girls called sophomores.
Oh! oh! I heard my roommate say
  That they were going to haze us.
     (Spoken:) (What's that, Ma?)
Boo! hoo! Boo! hoo! Boo! hoo!

January in Virginia.

TALL rose trees bend, with swelling buds agleam;
  The quaint red quince flowers flaunt their bits
    of flame;
Some strange white petals breathe a fragrance rare
Across the languor of the Southern air;
And graceful golden sprays of jasmine fall
In witching sunshine on the hidden wall.

The May-sprites must be dancing in the breeze;
The jasmine holds the magic of the Spring,
And sends me memories, longings, smiles, and tears,
Which only Northern violets used to bring.

                     LILIAN B. MINER.
The Youth's Companion,
  Jan. 22, 1891.

All-Hallow E'en.

'TIS Hallowe'en;
    The frosty sky is bright
    With deep-set gems.
The moon's kiss falls in sweet
Beneficence upon the earth.
Methinks it is a blessing
On our heads, my love,
        This Hallowe'en.

    'Tis Hallowe'en;
What spirits flit about
        On yonder wood,
Like shades upon the banks
Of silent Styx? You start, my sweet.
Nay, 'tis the oak tree parting
With their leaves. They sigh
        This Hallowe'en.

    'Tis Hallowe'en;
Bright Autumn's death is here,
        And Winter reigns.
But is it Death? Ah, no;
A holy rest and peace o'er all,

That yields its benediction
To our hearts, my love,
   This Hallowe'en.
                                    AGNES S. COOK.

An October Rose.

YET one more rose. One left, that Fall may know
The color, fragrance, zest, of Summer's show.
And ask'st thou why she lingers till the last,
When Summer's breath and Summer's blooms are past,
When Autumn beckons her with trembling hand,
And all about her dread forerunners stand?
And think'st thou 'tis past her time to glow,
   This last, late rose?

So long as suns shine warm and soft winds blow,
She blooms to let some hapless creature know
That Summer is not dead: just at a nap
She fell through drowsy chance from out her lap.
Can'st thou not read the message she would show,
   This last, sweet rose?

The Outlook,   CLARA BREWSTER POTWIN.
   October, 1893.

To Mt. Monadnock at Sunrise.

GRAY on thy crest the soft cloud curtains lie,
   Still guardians of thy morning slumbering.
Slow o'er thy head the star host marches by
   In state, and far beyond man's numbering.
The flocks repose upon thy quiet breast;
   All motionless they wait the coming day.
Thy somber rocks in shrouds of fog are drest
   As penitents who early rise and pray.
And now upon thy shadowy, wooded side,
   Amid the forests with their darkly dight,
Funeral plumes the king of shades doth hide,
   And sighs and moans the dying of the night.
But see! the stars in heaven grow more pale.
   Awake! and bid thy coming sovereign hail.

EVANGELINE KENDALL.

Exeunt.

RING down the purple curtains of the night!
   The play is played; the guests have gone away.
Why sit we staring at the empty stage,
The dying footlights, all the equipage
   Of motley fool and reveller, seen but gray
Where shadows hide the painted scenes from sight?

The play is played: come out into the dark!
   The far, white stars are burning in their place;
From mountain highlands blows a great, cool breath.
Art thou afraid? Nay, love, it is but death.
   Earth's masque is done. Lift up thine unchanged face!
Across the meadows sings the morning lark.

LILLIAN CORBETT BARNES.

Lippincott's Magazine,
   February, 1894.

Knighted.

ALL night within the dim cathedral choir
   He watched beside his armor: vigil kept
    With prayer and fasting, while his fellows slept;
And as the gray dawn touched the cross-capped spire,
There came to him a vision. Holy fire
   Of pure devotion up within him leapt,
   The song of service through his spirit swept,—
God's accolade bestowed on lowly squire.
When the sun shone across the world's new day
   They found him at the altar. Not a trace
    Of struggle on the fair, uplifted face;
     And, as they bore him home, they softly trod
With reverent feet, as those who go to pray.
   He died a squire: arise, O Knight of God!

MARY HOLLANDS McLEAN.

Beatrice Portinari.

O LADY with the calm and holy eyes
   Fixed ever steadfast on the Light Divine,
What happy fate, what noble lot was thine,
Thyself secure among the blest and wise,
To draw thy poet lover to the skies,—
   Teach him the secret meaning 'neath the sign,
   And lead, through realms where sun doth never shine,
His errant soul at last to Paradise?
Now in the clear effulgence of the day,
   Close drawn together by a deathless love,
Thou and thy Dante, glad, serene alway,
   The joy of being and its fullness prove.
O peace unmeasured, deep, and high and broad!
O hallowed union, perfected in God!

                                      MARY S. DANIELS.

Invited by Mistake.

A CALLOW youth received an invitation to the Prom;
He scarcely was acquainted with the maiden it was from;
But not the slightest difference did so small a matter make
Unto this luckless youth who was invited by mistake.

Chorus.

He will never forget the ices,
   He will never forget the cake;
But he'll always wish he hadn't been
   Invited by mistake.

A smiling usher brought him to a lady young and fair;
Though neither e'er had seen the other, what did either care?
An introduction might, thought he, this rare enjoyment break;
But she full soon divined he was invited by mistake.

They wandered through the corridors, and out beneath the sky;
He seemed a trifle spoony, and he heaved a pensive sigh.
He grew more sentimental as they neared the rippling lake;
He said the proper thing, although invited by mistake.

Oh! artfully she led him on,—this fresh and verdant youth;
She took some friends into the plot, and fun they had in sooth.
He thought she was a freshman, and, accordingly, he spake
Abundant foolishness, this man invited by mistake.

Still funnier he grew, and eke, he did facetiously
Make jokes about our rules, and e'en the sacred faculty;
But when she said "Good night," her words with horror made him quake:
"I am Professor Blank; you were invited by mistake."

SARAH JANE McNARY.

My Lord the Sun.

THE forests sway, and homage pay,
   As, rising from an eastern sea
Of rosy cloud the Sun shines proud.
   Largess of light he scatters free,
And showers around, with glory crowned,
   His rich regalia royally.

Lo! gray cloud-foes his path oppose,
   The monarch Sun of flight is fain;
In mist chained fast, his splendor past,
   He spreads imploring rays in vain.
The face of Day, his queen, droops gray,
   Tear-stained with drops of falling rain.

                          ISABELLA H. FISKE.

By the Roadside.

SHY violets among the tangled grass;
 Red robin, to thine own mate blithely singing,
Among the elm-tree boughs so gayly swinging,
My love, my true love, down this way will pass.

How shall you know her? By her sunny hair,
 Her grave, sweet eyes, all pure, no evil knowing:
 O robin! thou wilt turn to watch her going;
There is no maid in all the land so fair.

Shy violets among the tangled grass,
 Shed forth your richest perfumes 'neath her feet;
And gallant robin, when thou seest her pass,
 Trill out thy merriest lay her ears to greet;
And elm-tree branches, drooping low above her,
Whisper to her that I came by, and love her.

Louise R. Loomis.

Chaucer.

A STATELY lady's fair-haired little page;
  A "yong squyer," who rideth with a king;
  A poet taught of love and grief to sing
In sad strain and in sweet; whose heritage
Groweth the richer with increasing age,
  Till gladness, born of many dawns in spring,
  Fills all his soul, and merry notes outring
Along the road he fares on pilgrimage.
O blithest spirit of our English song!
  Down the far centuries floats thy happy lay,
    Untinged with cruel strife and restless pain;
Like a bird's carol, fresh, and free, and strong,
  It lifts its praise for life, and love, and May
    That blooms in sunshine after April rain.

Mary Hollands McLean.

Lake Waban.

THE hour is slow and still; and day and night
    Linger awhile together. How the glow
Fades in the west! How all the royal show
Shades to a dimmer glory, like the light
Of the flushed morn, but still subdued, less bright;
    And clear against the rose, the moon's thin bow
    Is set. A shadow creeps the earth below,
Tentative, following the feet of Night.
Ah, how the world is fair! Tired heart of mine,
    The little lake among the shadows there
Is the true poet; lifts her face, ashine
    With rose and the moon's silverness, more fair
Than evening's self. Here is the heart divine,
    Unspoiled by the dull weight of self-sought care.

S. VIRGINIA SHERWOOD.
At Wellesley.

Red Roses.

I ROAM in a garden, vestal fair,
The livelong, tranquil day,
Mid spotless lilies and snowdrops there,
   And tremulous tints of May;
Where myriad violets scent the gloom
   Of the forest-winding stream,
And throngs of white camellias bloom
   With a chill, unearthly gleam.
But I sicken of all, and cry to fate
For the red, red roses beyond the gate.

From every land, from every clime,
   The earth-stars here are come,
And proudly they banish the old lord Time
   From their glamour-haunted home.
But where the dreamful pansies grow,
   Uplifting their eyes to mine,
I wander restless, and sad, and slow,
   And seek for a flower divine.
Then I sicken of all, and cry to fate
For the red, red roses beyond the gate.

For there, from my vine-wreathed prison wall,
    I see their passionate glow;
I catch a fragrance rarer than all
    The breath of my flowers of snow.
The mystic light of their dusky hearts
    Strikes e'en my lilies dim;
And the wine of their beauty a fire imparts
    That thrills through brain and limb.
So I gaze in longing, and cry to fate
For the red, red roses beyond the gate.

"Beyond the gates," moans the wandering wind,
    "There are darker sights than these;
Freshness and bloom are hard to find,
    And the shade of Eden trees.
But the plains are bare and the mountains cold,
    And drear is the desolate sea;
The woe of the world is grim and old,
    'Tis death to thy flowers and thee."
But I hearken not: I cry to fate
For the red, red roses beyond the gate.

I know the sorrow, the gloom, and pain
    Of the world to a soul untried;

That my buds will wither, nor bloom again,
  If the gate be opened wide.
But I cry for freedom, for love, for life!
  For the real that conquers the dream!
And I know that there, in the heart of the strife,
  The victor's banners gleam.
So I break the bar, and fly with fate
To the red, red roses beyond the gate.

MARION PELTON GUILD.

A Rose.

I SAW it lying on the floor,
  The rose I gave her yesterday;
The little flower she prized no more
  Than just to wear, then throw away.

Its beauty gone, its fragrance sweet
  Spent all in vain upon the air;
I found it lying at my feet,
  Where it had fallen from her hair.

JOSEPHINE P. SIMRALL.

Alma Mater.

TO Alma Mater, Wellesley's daughters,
  All together join and sing;
Through all her wealth of wood and waters
  Let your happy voices ring.

In every changing mood we love her,
  Love her towers, and wood, and lake.
O changeful sky, bend blue above her;
  Wake, ye birds, your chorus wake!

We sing her praises now and ever,
  Blessèd fount of truth and love;
Our heart's devotion, may it never
  Faithless or unworthy prove.

We'll give our hearts and lives to serve her,
  Humblest, highest, noblest, all.
A stainless name we will preserve her,
  Answer to her ev'ry call.

ANNE BARRETT HUGHES.

Foiled.

THE sun had gone, and the shadowy night
  Had chased from the sky the last warm light,
When the waiting wind crept forth, and said,
"I will shake the reeds and the grasses dead,
And twist the boughs till they writhe and groan,
And the swaying pines shall wail and moan.
And I'll blow and blow where I please," cried he;
  "There is none to see."

Then the withered grasses were bended low,
And the quivering reeds shook to and fro,
While a sad wail came from the old pine tree,
And the wind laughed on, "There is none to see."
Then softly, O softly, so bright and still,
The wide-eyed moon came over the hill;
Came over and looked with her clear, full light
  Out into the night.

The telltale shadows began to move
As the moon kept watch from the hill above.
The baffled wind stood still; said he,
"If I twist the branches the moon will see,
And the shadows tell if I try to blow."

With a last low sigh he turned to go,
While the shadows still and the moon's full light
    Watched out the night.

                SARAH CHAMBERLIN WEED.

To One I Love.

CAN I tell you how I love you,
   With your beautiful brown eyes,
And your pretty lips, just parted,
   In a smile both sweet and wise?

No; I know I cannot tell you
   How the one warm spot you bring,
Gives my life, so cold and wintry,
   All the warmth of sunny spring.

Surely, I shall ne'er forget you
   Through life's mingled joy and care,
Darling little furry sable,
   That around my throat I wear!

                GERTRUDE JONES.

In Honorem: Henry F. Durant.

(Qui numquam quierit, quiescit.)

INTO what key shall glide the lingering strain—
The slow, sad minor that laments the dead?
Or the strong pæan, with exultant tread
Timing the march to victory and gain?
Shall the fond heart the happy past arraign,
Virtue on virtue, grace on grace, to plead,
Till whoso runs shall be constrained to read
The record of a work without a stain?
To the quick soul, past moments flung aside
No more like perishable vestments cling:
Success or failure lose their shame or pride,
And death, by Christ's sure balm, doth lose its sting.
But faith, and hope, and love,—these three abide:
His love, hope, faith,—these three alone we sing.

. . . .

However glad the days that we have spent,
We trust that gladder days are yet to be.
Crossing we know not what of land or sea,
In wealthier vineyards we shall pitch a tent,
With Eschol's heavier clusters downward bent.
And yet we need not think regretfully

Of him, our leader and our guide, for he
By faith had seen it all before he went.
From the slow-gathering shades wherein he stood,
He spake as the belovèd patriarch spake:
"I die,—but God shall visit you with good:
You shall go up, my children, and shall take
My prayer, my plan, my purpose for your sake,
Into your promised land of womanhood."
. . . .
"Let it be Christ's," he said; and yet again,
"Let it be Christ's": and this one choice was all.
Lesser desires, designs, may fail and fall,
However close unto the hearts of men;
May withering cling as shapely leaves do when
The growing stalk shoots upward straight and tall,
Rearing above the human-fashioned wall
Its heavenly blossom. Rudely, until then,
The leaf had typified the flower that came.
A friend's soft hand may pluck it now away
To treasure, or a hostile foot may blame
And trample: the same sap, the vital aim,
Climbs to the flower whereon all glances stay,
And none its fragrant symmetry gainsay.

MARY RUSSELL BARTLETT.

Apart.

I WOULD not call thee back to me to-night,
   Although my eager spirit turns to thee
With weary longing, and my eyes would see
Thy face aglow with spirit's power and might.
The sunset glow, the hillsides, every sight
   Of these familiar paths brings thoughts of thee.
   Thy name the maples whisper o'er to me,
Rustling their scarlet leaves in golden light.
Yet, though my heart doth yearn to have thee near,
   I will not call thee back. Love hath no end
Where daily intercourse alone is dear,
   Where spirit unto spirit cannot send
Its quickening power, though miles between us roll:
We still shall touch each other soul to soul.

     GERTRUDE SPAULDING HENDERSON.

Lullaby.

DREAMILY, dreamily swinging, swaying,
    Blow as the blossoms blow,—
Babekyn rocks in a faery cradle,
    Now high, now low.

Babekyn rocks in a faery cradle,
    Hung from the white moon's horn,
Pillowed on clinging, shimmering fleeces,
    From bright clouds shorn.

Gleefully, daintily swinging, swaying,
    Blossoms blow light in the wind;
Dawn-tinted petals fall thickly, till baby
    Is hard to find.

Wearily, wearily rocking, swaying,
    Even the robins rest;
When the sun is dead and the blossoms shiver,
    Long dreams are best.

                    EMILY S. JOHNSON.

H_2SO_4.

DIRECTIONS.

YOU take a few pieces of zinc,
   And put in your generator;
Add water, then plug in the cork,
   And pour in H_2SO_4.

OBSERVATIONS.

The action was not very brisk
   When I put in H_2SO_4,
So I tried nitric acid, to see
   If the thing wouldn't bubble up more.

CONCLUSIONS.

As I wiped up the acid and zinc,
   And swept up the glass from the floor,
I concluded I'd stick to directions,
   And try my own methods no more.

MARY ENO RUSSELL.

To an Oriole.

SWEETEST warbler of the Maytime,
   Rich thy liquid note, and rare!
Thou'rt a lover; I can tell it
   By thy bold, yet coaxing air.

'Tis thy loved one thou art calling
   To thy swinging dell aloft,
'Mid the blossoms Maytime opens,
   'Mid a fragance sweet and soft.

Now I see thee, orange-breasted,
   Flitting by on love intent;
Ah! thy song-tale is the sweetest
   Lover ere to loved one sent.

Blossom bower! Maytime fragrance!
   Subtle charm of lover's song!
Who resists you, who but loves you?
   Loves you fond, and loves you long!

ALMA E. BEALE.

Boating Song.

AWAY, away! more fleet than thought can follow,
>>Like a swallow
>Flies our wingèd boat along;
In measured strokes our strength the lithe oar bending,
>>Voices blending,
>Wake the echoes with our song.

REFRAIN.
Voices blending
With the waves in glad refrain
Wake the echoes with our strain.

Away, away! we leave the task enthralling.
>>Winds are calling,
>Morn is laughing in the sky;
Before our boat the blithe waves, quick retreating,
>>Timid greeting,
>Murmur as we hurry by.

Away, away! no thought of dull to-morrow:
>>Now we borrow
>Mirth and freedom from the day.
Each restless heart with calm and courage filling,
>>Hope instilling,
>Glide the careless hours away.

KENT DUNLAP HÄGLER.

To ———.

WE sat at the concert, she and I.
      She toyed with a rose;
      Her eyes glanced down;
      Her gown was brown.
         To its very close
      The song was of love—
      Deep love—that struggles,
That suffers, yet does not die.

Do you think she heard and felt its power,
        As, one by one,
      Down at her feet
      Fell the petals sweet,
         Till the song was done?
      That my heart lay, too,
    'Midst fragrance and song,
She knew,—yet toyed with her flower.

                MARY OTIS MALONE.

Mr. Edward Olney, Sir.

[Imitated by an Englishman in "Lady Clara Vere de Vere."]

MR. EDWARD OLNEY, sir,
    Of me you shall not win renown;
You thought to write an Algebra
    For pastime ere your sun went down.
You're not the child to draw it mild;
    The very Sphinx your pen inspired;
The father of an hundred woes,
    You are not one to be admired.

Mr. Edward Olney, sir,
    I know you proud to evolve your surds;
Your pride is yet no mate for mine,
    Too proud to count myself three thirds.
Nor would I break for your sweet sake
    A heart that bounds to truer glee;
A single line of Thomas Hood
    Is worth a dozen formulæ.

Mr. Edward Olney, sir,
    Some meeker pupil you must find,
For could I mete the Milky Way,
    I would not stoop to such a mind.

You sought to prove how I could cube,
    And my disdain is my reply;
Your stovepipe hat upon the nail
    Is not more stiff to you than I.

Mr. Edward Olney, sir,
    You bring strange sights before my eye;
Not thrice your birthday cakes have baked
    Since I beheld young Phœbe cry.
O, your curved lines! your minus signs!
    A great professor you may be,
But there was that upon her cheek
    Which you had hardly cared to see.

Mr. Edward Olney, sir,
    When thus she met her mother's view,
She had the passions of her kind, —
    She spake some certain truths of you;
Indeed, I heard one bitter word
    That scarce could justly be defined.
Her sentence lacked the accurate terms
    That stamp a mathematic mind.

Mr. Edward Olney, sir,
    A specter haunts your college walk:

The guilt of tears is at your door;
   You changed a wholesome heart to chalk.
You fixed the course without remorse,
   Regardless of her sore lament;
And when the day of trial came,
   You slew her with an eight per cent.

Trust me, Edward Olney, sir,
   Orion and the Pleiades,
From the blue heavens above us bent,
   Smile at your minutes and degrees.
Howe'er it be, it seems to me
   'Tis only fair ourselves to please;
Dry eyes are more than decimals,
   And happy hearts than indices.

I know you, Edward Olney, sir;
   You pine among your roots and powers:
The rolling light of your red eyes
   Is weary of the languid hours.
'Mid wondering trains, with boundless brains,
   But sickening of a vague disease,
You know so ill to factor time,
   You needs must play such pranks as these.

Edward, Edward Olney, sir,
   If time hangs heavy on your hands,
Are there no hinges off your gate,
   Nor any weeds upon your lands?
O, teach your little girl to bake,
   Or teach your little boy to hoe!
Pray Heaven for a human heart,
   And let the foolish freshman go.

KATHARINE LEE BATES.

Spiegel-Klarheit.
[From the German of Schultz.]

WHEN the Sun himself would mirror,
   He does not need the sea;
A reflector of his splendor
   E'en the smallest drop may be.
But the water clear as crystal
   Must be, whether drop or sea;
For the pure alone a mirror
   Of the pure can ever be,

ANNE BARRETT HUGHES.

By Waban Banks.

FLUTE of mine, break into song
    For the fleur-de-lis that throng
        Prisoned in the measure!
Add the whirr of butterfly,
Gnat, and spider, cruising by
        On their June-tide pleasure.

Let the prickly sedge have part
In the melody, its art,
        And the dimpling waters.
Filmy, gauze-bedappled things,
Bring them in with all their wings—
        Summer's sons and daughters.

Cicada and dragon fly,
Bees and beetled hosts awry,
        Grasshopper and cricket,
Locust and papilio,
Feathered moths that wander slow
        Through the ferny thicket.

Then a larger music roll:
Let it be the oriole,

    Let it be the plover,
    Kingfisher and secret thrush,
    Wren and blackbird—then a hush—

    Sing the rosy clover!
    Hymn the purple violet,
    Pitcher plants and meadows wet—
        Chant the marish reaches.
    —Pipe the gurgling, pleasant sound
    Of my least of boats, aground
        On the least of beaches.

              LILLIAN CORBETT BARNES.

Friendship.

MY garden, Lord, is filled with flowers,
    Roseate-hued or pale:
Some flowers needing sheltered bowers,—
Some, strong alone, like sun-lit towers.
    It is a needless tale
To tell to Thee their names—the measure
    Of life in each one's part.
Thou knowest all my garden treasure,
    Dear Lord! It is my heart.

              BERTHA PALMER.

Tides.

OH! the sea hath its ebb, and the sea hath its flow,
    And is ever the same great sea!
Now tossing their spray like the wreathèd snow,
    And laughing aloud in their glee,
In swift submission, glad, complete,
    That fills my soul with delight,
The strong waves cast them low at my feet,
    For now 'tis the tide's full height.

Last night the moon smiled fair and free,
    But the waves were all withdrawn,
And the line of foam shone filmily,
    Like a drifting cloud at dawn;
And long I paced the wet sea floor,
    With glimmering spoil o'erstrewn,
While the flood receded more and more,
    Like a vanishing, far-off tune.

So love hath its ebb, and love hath its flow,
    And is ever the same great love;
Through many a change our moon may go,
    But never can remove.

To-day, in full surrender sweet,
  It pours a lavish tide,
The breathless soul stands forth to greet,
  With eager arms flung wide.

Yestreen in silent, dark repose
  The conscious waters lay,
As if they fled pursuing foes,
  Or feared their queen's dear sway.
But never a doubt or a torturing pang,
  As I walked the shore, had I,
For "The sea is the sea," to myself I sang,
  "At low tide as at high."
JOSEPHINE A. CASS.

Life and Death.

L IFE is short;
  Death is long.
  Life's the prelude;
  Death's the song.

  The prelude is sweet,
    But the song ends never;
  Its music of peace
    Fills the vast forever.
MABEL A. CARPENTER.

The Passing Soul.

THE passing soul yearns forth from wistful eyes,
Whose solemn gaze is more than mortal-wise,
On death; and we who in the earthways fair
Held with her pace for pace—we may not share
That incommunicable, far surprise.

Yet must our grief-bewildered hearts surmise
How, with those slow-drawn, laboring, dying sighs
Time ebbs away, and yields to heavenly care
    The passing soul.

Our sorrow wanes from her, our living guise
Is dreamlike. Hushed in God's own hand she lies.
Deep in the valley of the shadow, there
His rod and staff they comfort her. We bear
The bitterness of death, but softly flies
    The passing soul.

KATHARINE LEE BATES.

The Night Wind in Winter.

IT toils unceasing, restless of all hope,
　A rushing sound that sweeps the universe,
Whirling a moan in rhythmical response
　　That swells out high, then mutters like a curse.

It seems at times the conscience of the world,
　That lives most keenly in the still of night,
To blast the hope that wrong may be forgot,
　And hound men on to some last work of might.

　　　　　　MARTHA HALE SHACKFORD.

At Sunset.

THE sun sinks down behind the firs,
　　The soft clouds hang beneath the sky
All gray and pink, like fairest pearls
　　That in far beds of Orient lie.

The distant hilltop glows with gold,
　　Within the valley shadows stray,
A sky all pink: a story told;
　　A blush where late a warm kiss lay.

　　　　　　EDITH E. TUXBURY.

A Senior Schedule.

WE'RE a-studying of Literature
    As hard as e'er we can;
We dote on Revolutions
    And the Brotherhood of Man.

We're returning to the People
    With a truly Lyric Cry;
And for Democratic Spirit
    We'd lay us down and die.

We're a-reading of Philosophy
    To find out why we be,
And a-learning that External Worlds
    Lie wholly in the Me.

We don't believe in Matter,
    And of Mind we're not quite sure;
We're inclined to think Uncertainties
    Most likely to endure.

We're a-studying Geology
    Of Pre-historic Times,

Before the Tides of Primal Sea
  Got written into rhymes;

When the "Old World spun forever,"
  And the poets never knew it,—
And all the Rocks, and Stones, and Things,
  Were nicely mixed up through it.

We're a-looking at Fine Pictures
  Made by People what are dead;
And we criticize Cathedrals
  With a Ruskin at our head.

We're a-growing awful learnèd,—
  There's lots more of the kind,—
But we do not mind confessing
  That it's all a Beastly Grind.

                MARY HOLLANDS MCLEAN.
"At Wellesley."

My Sophomore.

THERE is a Wellesley sophomore bright,
  As fair as a maid can be;
And in the lore of the days of yore
  There are few so skilled as she.
But oh! the grace of her winsome face
  Is more than her learnèd mind;
And to all, I own, save poor me alone,
  Most gracious she is and kind.

But oh! this Wellesley sophomore bright,
  Is as dull as a maid can be,
If with such a mind she cannot find
  How precious she is to me.
Yet dare I hope, when her powers have scope,
  And the scales fall at last from her eyes,
As she sees my love, and all doubts remove,
  'Twill be a delightful surprise?

ALICE WELCH KELLOGG.

The Song of the Lotus.

SLEEPILY, sleepily,
   Swaying and shifting,
Drowsily, drowsily,
   Nodding and drifting.
Odors of spicy balms,
Shadows of Eastern palms,
Cobwebs of phantasy,
   Twining and twisting.
Out of a melody
   Spinning soft slumbers,
Waving a mystery
   Into the numbers—
The river's full bosom
Beneath thee is swelling
   With passion's desire.
Out of the east, from
His full-orbèd dwelling,
Flings the moon-lover
   His passion's pure fire.

          JULIA STEVENS BUFFINGTON.

The Birthday in Heaven.

WHAT will they bring thee, Sweet, to-morrow's
    dawn,—
  Our three-year-old, whose birthday is in heaven?
For the earth-happiness thou hast foregone
  What will they do to make the balance even?
Do the grave angels love as mothers love?
  And is there one, just one from all the rest,
Whose arms were first to cradle thee above,
  To whom thou turnest, whom thou lovest best?

Yea, surely mother-hearts in heaven must beat,
  Else 'twere not heaven, and God were God no
    more:
Could he be happy in his holy seat
  If any child stood homesick near the door?
Tell that dear angel that doth keep our child
  To hold thee close to-morrow, and to press
Upon thy brow, grown radiantly mild,
  All that we would of lingering caress.

Tell her on earth we brought thee toys and flowers,
  And told thee stories when thy birthday came;

Say to her that when thou wast wholly ours,
  With love unspeakable we called thy name;
And when the shadows fell,—rememberest thou?—
  How thou didst nestle down in sheltered sleep!
Who sings to thee? Whose arms infold thee now?
  To whom has God my jewel given to keep?

Be not unhappy, Sweet. Enjoy her care;
  Go to her first of all the heavenly host;
But, oh, do not forget me, is my prayer!
  I am thy mother; love me still the most.

MARY WRIGHT PLUMMER.

A New=Year's Wish.

MAY the new year be friendly and loving,
  And guide thee a gentle way,
And with hands like an eager lover's,
  Bring thee some new gladness each day.

CLARA BREWSTER POTWIN.

Love Song.

Dearest, my heart is full of love,
    But I cannot speak it to-day,
For the light is gone from the sky above,
    And the clouds are all dark and gray.

Dearest, my heart is full of pain,
    But I hide it deep out of sight,
For sunshine is filling the sky again,
    And the world is aglow with light.

JOSEPHINE P. SIMRALL.

I wonder if the dying leaf
    Feels any hint of pain;
I wonder if the with'ring rose
    Longs to be fresh again.

I've wondered, too, if daisies white
    Straight under summer sun,
Or tossed in rain above the dust,
    Hope that their life is done.

MARTHA HALE SHACKFORD.

A Second Thought.

IN the ancient days
    Arthur loved his queen;
Guinevere loved Arthur not,
Lost in love for Lancelot.

Love is passing sweet,
Men and maidens say;
But I know that Guinevere
Seeking joy, found wild-eyed fear.

If, dear, one should think you
Somewhat cold and high,
One would be wise to ponder well
That seeking fire, one might find hell.

                              FLORENCE WILKINSON.
The Century Magazine,
    January, 1896.

A Tree-day Song.

A SONG of the spring, a rhyme
With a merry, musical chime
Ringeth abroad to-day,
Sweet old song of the May!
Shy little flowers, peep through!
This is the time for you.
Listen to hear the rest
From the oriole in the nest!

Chorus.

Out of the old is the new,
Under the storm is the blue.
For each little leaf of the tree
Shall the warm May sunshine be.
Fairer the summer in store
Than all the summers before.

Hear the song of our tree!
Long is its pedigree.
Centuries come and go,
Strong and stern in the snow

Stand the forests of beech,
Winter and summer for each.
Listen to hear the rest
From the bird of the crimson breast!

Who needeth a song? Not we;
Ours is the song of the tree.
Ours is the song of the May;
Sing it and say it to-day!
Old is the earth in truth—
A dream of the past its youth.
The sun is low in the west,
But listen to hear the rest.

ANNIE JERRELL TENNEY.

Corot.
(Ars omnis est una.)

O POET-PAINTER, steeped in Art,
  Thy brush has only been thy pen.
Had that been lost thee, then thou must
  Have *sung* thy soul out to us men.

CLARA BREWSTER POTWIN.

An Irish Boat Song.

THE dark o' the night was comin' fast,
For 'twas avenin' afther tay was past,
An' jist the time when boatin's swate,
An' gals come down all dressed so nate,
Bay jabbers.

The capn's were followin' after the rist,
A runnin' down hill like all possist,
An like an old tin fish-horn rung
The accints of the freshmen tongue,
Bay jabbers.

The sophs are a watchin' 'em up on the shore;
First up goes one, thin another oar,—
Boats goin' this way, thin goin' that,
An' now one crayture's lost her hat,
Bay jabbers.

"Pick up that hat," the cap'n said,
An' jam it quick on the top o' yer head;
For the way is long, and the lake is wide,
And the boats must be hauled up side by side,
Bay jabbers.

Steer shy o' that sailboat out on the lake,
Or your fayther'll be telegraphed to a wake.
That's Hunnewell's boat, there's a man inside,
An' ye must kape up the college pride,
       Bay jabbers.

Wait a bit now, says one, and rist,
For the dress I have on is my very bist;
An' the boat has a lake, an' the wather's high,
An' I'll jist haul it up to kape it dry,
       Bay jabbers.

The bell is ringin' for half past seven,
From six till thin is the time that's given;
An' they'll have to row at an awful rate
To be at the bell at a quarther of eight,
       Bay jabbers.

But with all their rowin' they don't get in;
So jist to punish them for their sin
They lock them out of the beautiful gate,
Cos they're not in at quarther of eight,
       Bay jabbers.

So they sit thim down on the cold stone steps,
As if they were nothin' but common Preps;
And nobody comes to let thim in,
But lave them there to repint of their sin,
                         Bay jabbers.

        AMBIA C. HARRIS, CLARA A. JONES.

A Song of Praise.

WHEN foes too strong my spirit vex,
    And meet me at a thousand ways,
I boldly lift my voice and sing
    A song of praise.

    So much of good the Father sends,
        So many mercies crown my days,
    I'll aye have reason to prolong
        This song of praise.

The powers of ill can ne'er endure
    A heart attuned to grateful lays;
Like shades at dawn they flee before
    My song of praise.

                      FLORENCE E. HOMER.

Isolation.

THINKEST thou that a great distance
   Lies between thee and yon star?
Thy soul's friends, the best and dearest,
   In their nearness are as far.

CHARLOTTE ROSE STANLEY.

Consolation.
[In reply to " Isolation."]

LOOK! Seest thou yon bright star-beam,
   E'en tho' distant, pierce the night?
Ray divine, thy dear one's friendship,
   Thro' thy darkness, is as bright.

AGNES E. WOOD.

Vivisection.

IF vivisection merely
   Afflicted dogs, and such,
Although it would be shocking,
   It wouldn't hurt so much
As when a human *coeur* is rent
   In twain by human touch.
I pray you then have mercy
   On me, a lover true,
Whose heart, in bleeding sections,
   Is carried off by you.

FRANCES C. LANCE.

A Senior's Compliment.

'TWAS Saturday night. Three seniors tall
   Upon a freshman went to call.
"What a lovely room!" the first one sighed.
"A perfect gem!" number two replied.
The third just glanced at the fresh, young face,—
"No gem," said she, "but a jewel case."

Le Pays du Tendre.
[Rondel.]

LAND of the madrigal and ode,
   Of rainbow air and cloudless weather,—
Tell me, what ferny, elfin road
   Will lead my eager footsteps thither?

Trick'd out in gems shall I go hither?
   And in a carriage *à la mode*,
Land of the madrigal and ode,
   Of rainbow air and cloudless weather?

Or in the garb by Love bestow'd,
   With roses crowned, and sprays of heather,
With mandolin and dart embow'd,
   Shall Cupid and I go together—
Land of the madrigal and ode,
   Of rainbow air and cloudless weather?

                    ABBE CARTER GOODLOE.

Her Second Degree.
[A Tenor Solo.]

SHE was a Wellesley senior;
   The time, Commencement Day;
The spot,—nor wood, nor water
   Will e'er her trust betray;
For there a gracious future
   Stood forth in glory dressed,
And in the vision promised
   To answer her behest.
That selfsame day I rose from earth,
   And, poised in Harvard sky,
I promptly caught each wingèd thought
   That fain would pass me by.

Exultantly they carolled—
   These tho'ts that flew so high—
"Farewell, O work domestic,
   I leave thee here to die.
I go to sweep the shadows
   From human nature's sky;
My life, my love, my freedom,
   No single heart can buy.

Alone I search the world for truth,
  I kneel at no man's feet;
She raiseth none who kneels to one,—
  My being stands complete.

"To this old rugged earth-ball
  I pledge my service here,
Until the world, remoulded,
  Rolls on a perfect sphere.
Then Alma Mater proudly
  Shall call me to her side,
And say, 'Your greatness, daughter,
  Is as the ocean wide;
In token slight of deep regard
  This parchment take from me.'
Heart, soul, and mind spent for mankind,
  Shall win my second degree."

A dozen years have flitted;
  That senior, as my bride,
Has found the world less rugged
  Since trav'ling by my side;
Her dearest work domestic
  Is for our children three.

Alas, must I disclose it,
"Mankind" means chiefly me,
Tho' Wellesley has not called her yet,
  Nor will, that I can see,—
The handmaid still of love's sweet will,
  She's won her Second Degree, M—A.

FRANCES C. LANCE.

SHALL I tell you of my lover,
    Brave and true?
All his hidden charms discover
    To your view?
Shall I tell you of his sweetness,
Of his rich and full completeness?
But I can't until I meet him;
    Now, could you?

THEODORA KYLE.

Crossing the Ocean.

SWISH-SWASH! Swish-swash!
Over my head and at my feet
I hear the water's restless beat,
And here I'm going up, up, up;
But before I'm up, I'm down,
And I wonder, wonder where I am,
As I gaze about with a frown.
On a shelf in a box I seem to be laid,
And I query, half afraid,
Am I freight, or am I human?
Am I fish, or am I woman?
External tumult, internal commotion,—
Tell me, can this be crossing the ocean?

CHARLOTTE FITCH ROBERTS.

Easter.

THE sun, arising in the day's glad dawning,
    Shines on the flowers with his most tender rays;
They know his power, and, waking, feel its warning,
    And turn their faces to his light in praise.

O Sun of Righteousness, above us shining,
    So strong in power, yet gentle in thy grace,
Thou dost arise on souls in darkness pining,
    And all the world must turn to meet thy face!

SARA COOLIDGE BROOKS.

A Touch.

YOU are holding a soul in your delicate fingers;
    O cradle it well!
For the odor of leaves and the rose-touch lingers
    Where the rose-leaf fell.

FLORENCE ANNETTE WING.

Never a Day Without a Cloud.

HOWEVER so fair the day may be,
Some tiny cloud we can always see;
Some shadow will flit across the sky;
Some dark-winged messenger will draw nigh.
And so we sigh for the perfect day,
When the sun shall shine with undimmed ray,
Forgetting that all we so dearly prize
In the morning hour or the sunset skies,
The beauty that sets our hearts aglow,
Without the clouds, we never might know;
Forgetting the summons to life they bring
To the waiting seed in the dark earth's spring;
Forgetting that fruit from flower we gain,
When blossoms have fallen in wind and rain;
Forgetting, alas! that the pathway bright
With heavenly promise, appears in sight
Alone when the tears of the rain fall fast,
And the sun's great glory has through them passed.

DELIA MARIA TAYLOR.

The Lake-Singer.

OUT on the lake a note I heard,—
A note as of a random bird;
Now loud it was, now low, now high,
Now dying, on the dying wind.
The wind itself seemed loath to die
And leave so sweet a sound behind.

The sun below the hill sank, red,
A crown of glory on his head;
A purple cloud, through streaks of light,
Sailed, dreaming, toward the dreaming North,
While forms of majesty and might
Against the blue were shadowed forth.

The lake itself lay dark and deep,
Hushed like a child when half asleep.
Gray-blue beneath the gray-blue arch
A little boat, with rippling sound,
Stole from the shadow of a larch
Into the evening-calm, profound.

Again that sound upon the lake!
A shivering echo, half awake,
Moans from the purple sunset-hill;
A softened swishing round the boat—
Again that unexpected trill,
An eastern nightingale afloat!

The sun is gone, the shadows rise,
The color fades from darkening skies,
The single boat hath reached the shore,
A single star appeareth bright;
The single singer sings no more,—
The lake is wrapped in silent night.

KATE WATKINS TIBBALS.

In College Days.

WHAT golden ways,
    Those college days,
We rode and rode together!
    Leaving behind
    The weary grind,
We wheeled away with lightsome mind
    From cap and gown,
    From student-frown,
Into the autumn weather.

    Glowing with sense
    Of life intense,
And zest of life wild-hearted,
    Above, we knew
    The sky was blue,
So on we flew, and on we flew,
    The while the air,
    A champagne rare,
Our sleeping pulses started.

On, spinning faster,
We saw the aster
Its frosted purples fling
By wayside wall,
And over all
The woodbine weave its scarlet shawl;
And, dimmed its gold
At touch of cold,
The golden-rod upspring.

Then, musing, slow
We used to go
When distant far from town;
And on the wold
Leaves manifold
Fell, carpeting our way with gold.
How loth they fell
I mind me well,
How sadly circled down!

Cathedral shades
The woodland glades
Drew down upon our roaming,

As, homeward turned,
The ground we spurned,
While one white star above us burned;
And mystic-sober
Became October
Gray in the quiet gloaming.

Such golden ways,
Those college days,
We rode in sun and breeze;
We left behind
The weary grind,
And wheeled away with lightsome mind,
Finding anew
The golden, true
Fabled Hesperides.

FLORENCE WILKINSON.

List of Contributors.

Margaret Steele Anderson, '87-88	16
Lillian Corbett Barnes, B.A., '91	69, 97, 124
Mary Russell Bartlett, B.A., '79	18, 74, 112
Katharine Lee Bates, B.A., '80, M.A., '91	13, 26, 38, 120, 128
Alma E. Beale, B.A., '91	75, 117
Mary Allison Bingham, B.A., '79	80
Sara Coolidge Brooks, B.A., '85	150
Julia Stevens Buffington, B.S., '94	133
Isabella Campbell, B.S., '94	83
Mabel A. Carpenter, '94-95	33, 127
Josephine A. Cass, B.A., '80	14, 57, 126
Mabel Wing Castle, B.A., '87	51
Florence Converse, B.S., '93	50
Agnes S. Cook, '91-92	94
Mary S. Daniels, B.A., '86, M.A. (McMaster Univ.), '94	99
Isabella H. Fiske, B.A., '96	102
Nancy K. Foster	91
Abbe Carter Goodloe, B.S., '89	17, 145
Cornelia E. Green, B.A., '92	15, 30, 73
Marion Pelton Guild, B.A., '80	43, 106
Kent Dunlap Hägler, B.A., '90	76, 118
Ambia C. Harris, '81	140
Mary Hefferan, B.A., '96	19, 87
Gertrude Spaulding Henderson, B.S., '92	114
Florence E. Homer, B.S., '86	29, 142
Anne Barrett Hughes, B.S., '87	109, 123
Emily S. Johnson, '97	115
Clara A. Jones, B.A., '80	22, 140

Gertrude Jones, B.A., '95 111
Alice Welch Kellogg, B.A., '94 . . . . . 64, 88, 132
Evangeline Kendall, B.A., '96 96
Ada May Krecker, B.A., '95 . . . . . . 41, 56
Theodora Kyle, B.A., '91 148
Frances C. Lance, B.S., '92 . . . . . . 144, 146
Anna Robertson Brown Lindsay, B.A., '83, M.A., '88,
    Ph.D., '92 . . . . 25, 84
Louise R. Loomis, '97 103
Martha Gause McCaulley, B.A., '88 37
Mary Hollands McLean, B.A., '96 . . . . 49, 98, 104, 130
Sarah Jane McNary, B.A., '90, M.A. (Univ. of City of
    N. Y.), '92 100
Mary Otis Malone, '98 119
Lillian B. Miner, B.A., '88 93
Helen Barrett Montgomery, B.A., '84 . . . . . 20, 62
Bertha Palmer, B.A., '91, M.A., '93 125
Mary Wright Plummer, '81-82 . . . . . 34, 72, 134
Clara Brewster Potwin, B.A., '84 . . . . . 95, 135, 139
Lillian B. Quinby, B.A., '94 . . . . 36, 70
Katharine Mordantt Quint, B.A., '90 41
Charlotte Fitch Roberts, B.A., '80, Ph.D. (Yale), '94 . . 149
Helen Worthington Rogers, B.A., '92, M.A., '93 . . . 68
Mary Eno Russell, B.A., '80 116
Martha Hale Shackford, B.A., '96 . . . . . 129, 136
S. Virginia Sherwood, B.A., '96 105
Josephine P. Simrall, B.S., '93 . . . . . 40, 82, 108, 136
Charlotte Rose Stanley, B.A., '88 . . . . . 28, 63, 143
Harriot Brewer Sterling, B.S., '86 90
Josepha Virginia Sweetser, B.A., '90 . . . . . 54, 78
Delia Maria Taylor, B.A., '82, M.A., '87 151
Annie Jerrell Tenney, '82 138
Maud Thompson, '94 71
Kate W. Tibbals, '99 152
Edith E. Tuxbury, B.S., '94 129

Sarah Chamberlin Weed, B.A., '95 . . . . . 21, 89, 110
Mabel W. White 77
Florence Wilkinson, B.A., '92 . . . . . . 66, 137, 154
Florence Annette Wing, B.A., '92 . . . . . 42, 150
Anna Estelle Wolfson, '99 52
Agnes E. Wood 143
Ada S. Woolfolk, B.S., '91 60

www.ingramcontent.com/pod-product-compliance
Lightning Source LLC
Chambersburg PA
CBHW030314170426
43202CB00009B/1002